The Conversation Manager

The power of the modern consumer, the end of the traditional advertiser

STEVEN VAN BELLEGHEM

KoganPage

LONDON PHILADELPHIA NEW DELHI

The masculine pronoun has been used in this book. This stems from a desire to avoid ugly and cumbersome language, and no discrimination, prejudice or bias is intended.

First published in 2010 in Belgium by Lannoo Campus Publishers, Erasme Ruelensvest 179 bus 101, B-3001 Leuven (België)
www.lannoocampus.com

First published in Great Britain and the United States in 2012 by Kogan Page Limited

120 Pentonville Road	1518 Walnut Street, Suite 1100	4737/23 Ansari Road
London N1 9JN	Philadelphia PA 19102	Daryaganj
United Kingdom	USA	New Delhi 110002
www.koganpage.com		India

© Steven Van Belleghem, 2012

The right of Steven Van Belleghem to be identified as the author of this work has been asserted by him in accordance with the Copyright, Designs and Patents Act 1988.

ISBN   978 0 7494 6659 6
E-ISBN   978 0 7494 6660 2

British Library Cataloguing-in-Publication Data

A CIP record for this book is available from the British Library.

Library of Congress Cataloging-in-Publication Data

Van Belleghem, Steven.
   The conversation manager : the power of the modern consumer, the end of the traditional advertiser / Steven Van Belleghem.
      p. cm.
   Includes bibliographical references.
   ISBN 978-0-7494-6659-6 – ISBN 978-0-7494-6660-2   1. Marketing–Social aspects.
2. Internet marketing–Social aspects.   3. Customer relations.   4. Social media.
5. Management–Social aspects.   I. Title.
   HF5415.V283 2012
   658.8–dc23   2012003188

Typeset by Graphicraft Ltd, Hong Kong
Print production managed by Jellyfish
Printed and bound by CPI Group (UK) Ltd, Croydon, CR0 4YY

Contents

Thanks and acknowledgements

You never write a book alone. Without the help and encouragement of many people, this particular story would never have reached the printing presses.

During recent years, I have had the pleasure and good fortune to work with a team of passionate and innovative people. My thanks in the first instance therefore go to the management team of InSites Consulting: Tim, Joeri, Niels, Kristof, Christophe, Sam and Filip. If you are writing a book, it is highly motivating to know that your company is prepared to give you the necessary time and space to do it full justice. Thank you for believing in me and my story.

Thanks, too, to all the other staff at InSites Consulting who have contributed in whatever manner, great or small, to the finished text. Feedback on a presentation; the passing on of a useful link; the placing of an article on the internal knowledge platform; a story about a brand experience: one way or another, they have all helped to inspire me. It is an honour to work with such a caring, sharing team. Thank you everybody!

But our team was not my only source of inspiration. Over the years, many customers have offered us the chance to grow in this fascinating research domain. This has given me the luxury of gaining insights into the workings of many interesting companies, and provided the yeast to the gradual fermentation of my Conversation Manager ideas. My special thanks go to Hans Schmeits, Rene Hansen, Rudi Van Campenhout and Catherine Franeau (UCB), Alexis Bortoluzzi (Goodyear), Kristin Blondé, Lode Hoste and Kim Gils (VMMa), Catherine Herssens (Unilever), Chris Ven (Pfizer), Sabien Deboodt (Sanofi Pasteur MSD), Debbie Bogaert (Friesland Campina), Mieke Quintyn and Philippe Orban (Belgacom). Thanks also to Peter Quaghebeur (director-general, VMMa) and Jo Nachtergaele (marketing director, VMMa), Erwin Deckers (programme director, Q-music), Erik Van Vooren (manager, DM Institute) and Evarist Moonen (commercial director, FC Bruges) for their equally inspirational conversations.

It is with pleasure that I thank Professor Rudy Moenaert, who has been a never-ending source of inspiration to me. His incisive and enquiring mind provided me with new energy when I was flagging and new insights when I needed them most. Thanks for the inspiration, Rudy – and also for writing the foreword.

My first work experience was at the Vlerick Leuven Ghent Management School. After I made the step across to InSites Consulting, I continued to lecture at the school. This gave me the opportunity to test my ideas on many experienced and well respected marketeers. I will always be grateful to the school for this opportunity.

To Hilde Van Mechelen, Petere Saerens and Lieven Sercu (Lannoo Publishers), I would like to say thank you for believing in this project. I have always valued your advice and your ever-constructive criticism. I would also like to thank Pascal Van Hoorebeke for the graphical design of the book. Towards Paul Nola, thanks for the detailed pre-read of the English version of the book.

And last but not least, the biggest thank you of all goes to my wife Evi. During the past few years, she has constantly encouraged me to develop my story of the Conversation Manager. I wrote the book during her pregnancy, and I am still not sure which of us needed the most support: her or me! Thanks for everything Evi!

Foreword

It is 27 September 2009, at roughly half-past five in the afternoon. Cadel Evans, a man 'born to lose', has just won the World Cycling Championship in Mendrisio. This comes as a surprise to both outsiders and insiders, as the comments of the Belgian television commentary team make clear. In passing, they also inform me that this is the first ever Australian world title on the road. At around six-fifteen I check *Wikipedia* to see how other countries score in this respect. Belgium still heads the list with 25 victories, followed by Italy with 19. Holland (our traditional cycling rival) has just 7! But my biggest 'aha'-moment is when I see that *Wikipedia* has already been updated. Cadel Evans is already listed as the winner for 2009 and Australia already stands proudly in the list of championship winning countries. Who are these internauts who live in the *intense lane* of the information highway and who are offering the world a new élan? This is a battle that *Encyclopedia Britannica* can never win.

'Always in motion is the future', declares Yoda in *The Empire Strikes Back*. This declaration (albeit somewhat ungrammatically) puts its finger on the problem facing today's modern managers, consultants and academics in the internet era. The future is unfolding faster than the past can be evaluated and appreciated. My favourite shopping site, *Amazon.com*, is packed with books which can never live up to people's level of expectation. How far and for how long can we carry on limping behind the past? Where is the paradigm shift that will allow us to give meaning to this past and still extract maximum benefit from the future?

The Conversation Manager provides this breakthrough. The author, Steven Van Belleghem, has written a brilliant analysis of how the internet will alter *your* commercial strategy. He does this with great style and bravura, which gave me the comfortable feeling that I was the pupil in the presence of a great master! His activities at InSites Consulting – a successful internet start-up which expertly combines science and market research – have given him the opportunity to examine at close quarters the work of the *digizens* who cruise along the information highway. *The Conversation Manager* is a remarkable piece of work – and one that you will enjoy reading. I hope you won't mind if I give you a brief summary of the book's structure, using three legendary *YouTube film* clips as my guide.

Part One reminded me of the *Did you know?* clip, in which you can learn (amongst other things) that in just one (!) week the *New York Times* offers you more information than someone in the 18th century was able to process and absorb in their entire lifetime. The general tone of *Did you know?* is ominous and the Fat Boy Slim rap '*Right here, right now*' is prominent in the mix. Steven Van Belleghem goes for a different approach. His 'did-you-knows' are never threatening. He explains tectonic shifts in the internet landscape, yet manages to convey them to his readers with humour and style. Simple words and easily recognizable examples illustrate and soften the impact of these seismic changes at the deeply human and emotional level of 'you' and 'I'. Whether he is talking about Oprah Winfrey, Domino's pizza or FC Bruges (his favourite football team), one conclusion remains inescapably in the foreground: authenticity is the trump card in the global brand village of the modern marketeer. The virtual world is not developing alongside everyday reality, but right at its very heart.

It is not possible to bypass – let alone win – the modern commercial chess game with the logic of the past. Forget 'either...or'. Think 'and'... 'and'. The modern marketeer needs to sense emotionality and control rationality; value the individual and steer society in the direction he wants. In Part Two Steven Van Belleghem openly approaches the question of what we must do to achieve brand identification in the 21st century. He never lapses into cheap and easy theorizing, but is practical and concrete at all times. This part reminds me of the powerful *Last Lecture* by Randy Pausch. What would you do if you knew that this was your very last chance to act? Doing nothing is not an option. Laziness could be lethal! The solution is as simple as it is challenging, as obvious as it is powerful: marketeers must become Conversation Managers. The use of capital letters is not just a nice stylistic touch: it serves to underline the importance of these new players in your new commercial organization. The Conversation Manager is a strong personality who listens to and talks to consumers.

And then it is time to start your own personal journey. Or to put it another way: after you have read Part One and Part Two, you will be positively burning to start your journey. This book gives me the same feeling as when I first saw the clip *Where the hell is Matt?* on *YouTube* in 2008. Matt danced to a catchy tune and the evocative poetry of

Rabindranath Tagore at places in the world where I also wanted to be. In a similar way, Steven writes about things that I want to do. In fact, I am desperate to try them all out! Part Three is a real *tour de force*: he tells us how we can all become Conversation Managers (you will note that I have deliberately adopted his capital letters trick). Simple propositions, simply put, but beautifully illustrated with clear and telling examples (like me, you will certainly remember the idea of the McDonald's discount voucher in Burger King!).

Good books fill up the gaps in our knowledge. Very good books change our way of thinking. Exceptional books change our way of life. This is an exceptional book. It is destined – and rightly – to join the list of best-sellers by such international stars as Seth Godin, Jack Trout or Malcolm Gladwell. In our modern world, innovations are global and ideas are democratic, in the broadest sense of the word. *The Conversation Manager* offers us all crystal-clear insights and usable advice. The familiarity of many of the Dutch and Flemish examples makes the book highly accessible for readers in the Benelux: hopefully our other readers will find them interesting as well. Be that as it may, Van Belleghem's arguments are skilfully put, scientifically based and backed up by razor-sharp synthesis at the end of each chapter. This book is the marketing equivalent of *Back from the future!* Like a latter-day Michael J. Fox, Steven Van Belleghem shows us the way to our future. In short, this book gave me – to use one of Steven's own quotes – 'answers to the questions I never even knew I had'.

The Conversation Manager is the story of a voyage of discovery, told in a fascinating manner by a guide who has already reconnoitred the pathways to the future which he now advises us to follow. My final conclusion is simple: *The Conversation Manager* is written by a true *Conversation Champion*. I wish this book the success that it so richly deserves.

Rudy Moenaert
Professor of Strategic Marketing –
TiasNimbas Business School

Catch me if you can

Ever heard of the story of Frank Abagnale Junior?

Frank Abagnale is one of the most famous confidence tricksters in the history of the United States. Between his sixteenth and his twenty-second birthdays, he was able to persuade dozens of otherwise sensible people that he was variously a pilot, a lawyer, a professor and a paediatrician. At the same time, he also managed to 'earn' a cool 2.5 million dollars from forged cheques. He was always too smart for the people he was trying to con – and for the people who were trying to catch him. Frank Abagnale had the rare ability to transform his appearance and his personality with a flexibility of which your average chameleon would be proud. For many years, he was able to give the FBI the run-around. But as time passed, the FBI gradually became smarter as well. In the end, they were able to track Frank Abagnale down, and with the help of the French police he was arrested.

End of story – or so you might think. But you would be wrong!

Five years after Abagnale was sent to prison, he received a strange proposition – from the American government that had arrested him! They wanted his help. Some bright spark in the FBI realized that Frank would be the ideal person to help them catch other confidence tricksters and frauds – particularly the financial fraudsters, who were costing the government millions of dollars each year in lost tax revenue. For Frank, it was an offer he couldn't refuse. It was certainly better than sitting out the rest of his lengthy sentence. In the meantime, Frank has been working for the Feds for more than 30 years. More than 14,000 financial institutions, private companies and government departments have made use of his anti-fraud expertise. In 1998 he was invited by CNN Financial News to become a member of 'Pinnacle 400', a group of 400 specialists who are right at the very top of their profession.

Perhaps this story has a familiar ring to it? It was filmed as *Catch Me If You Can*, based on the best-selling book of the same title and starring Leonardo Di Caprio and Tom Hanks.

The storyline, which follows the cat-and-mouse game played out between the con-man and his pursuers, is a perfect metaphor for the challenge facing today's advertisers. Consumers use the power of the internet to maximum effect. They realize that their own impact on society is increasing. The only way to deal successfully with this new phenomenon is to do what the American government did when it decided to turn to Frank Abagnale for help. By picking Frank's brains, the FBI created a lever effect which allowed them to unmask dozens of other fraudsters. This lever would never have been available if Abagnale had been locked up in the slammer for the rest of his days.

The challenge for us, as advertisers and managers, is to find this kind of lever with consumers. Allow them to contribute to the build-up of your brand.

In this book, *The Conversation Manager*, I will explain why traditional-style advertising no longer works. There is a need for change in the manner in which we carry out our day-to-day work. Hopefully, I will be able to offer solutions which will enable us to meet these new challenges.

The First Part examines the growing gulf between modern consumers and traditional advertisers. In recent years, the internet has developed at lightning speed, evolving from a static platform into a social platform. This evolution has had an impact on the manner in which consumers communicate their purchasing decisions. Unfortunately, most advertisers have failed to realize this. They are standing still, instead of moving forward. As a result, the gulf has continued to grow, and now poses a serious threat to their profession. Certainly now that a new generation of advertisers is on the horizon.

Part Two begins to sketch the first outlines of a possible solution. I will elaborate a change pathway which will transform the 20th-century advertiser into a 21st-century Conversation Manager. During this change process, the Conversation Manager will refocus on brand identification, advertising and... conversations (what else did you expect from a Conversation Manager?). The resulting relationship between your brand and the consumer should act as the lever to improve your sales results.

But I am looking to provide more than a theoretical framework. The book will also offer a number of practical tools which will allow you to start your change process within the first 48 hours. Part Three will outline a number of concrete tips that can be used to adjust your company strategy in the direction of Conversation Management. And there will be plenty of handy online-tools to help you with your new job: the fascinating job of the Conversation Manager.

The basis of the book

*T*he Conversation Manager* is based on four years of research by the team at InSites Consulting, supplemented with insights gleaned from a thorough investigation of the relevant professional literature, conversations with advertisers, projects for customers, the many reactions to our workshops and seminars, and (how could it be otherwise) my own visions and beliefs.

Good luck on your fascinating journey of self-discovery and change!

Steven Van Belleghem

Part One
Together
we are strong

PART ONE CONTENTS

Chapter One
The power of
the modern consumer

Before we start...

This chapter will tell you that consumers have not changed as much as some people have claimed. However, in recent years consumers have discovered the possibilities offered by the internet. This tool seems to be a facilitator for various human characteristics. As a result, some of these characteristics have become magnified, and so have assumed a greater importance in consumer make-up.

Although much has already been written on these matters, it is important to discuss some of the most important qualities of the contemporary consumer, in order to strengthen the Conversation Manager's theoretical frame of reference. In this way, the contrast between the evolution of the consumer (Chapter 1) and the status-quo of marketing (Chapter 2) will be made clear.

The consumer has not changed... much

People have always influenced each other in terms of the purchase of goods and services. Ever since commercial trading first began, people have been formulating positive and negative opinions about buying and selling, and the people who carry it out. Your friendly, neighbourhood baker is doing good business because the local people recommend him to their family, friends and acquaintances. Well-reputed restaurants are fully booked, while poor restaurants often have more staff than customers. Positive recommendations result in the positive evolution of your trading activities, whether you are selling bread or Michelin-star gastronomy. So much is obvious.

In 1944 the concept of *word-of-mouth* (WOM for short) was first included in the scientific investigation of marketing and advertising. Paul Lazarsfeld[1] concluded that the mass media (newspapers, TV, radio) are not able to influence the decision-making processes of a consumer to a level of 100 per cent. It was certainly true, he agreed, that the mass media are usually the first channel by which consumers become aware of new products. But Lazarsfeld's research suggested that this initial factor alone is insufficient to explain the consumer's buying behaviour. In a second phase, consumers talk to each other about the new products they have seen advertised. By exchanging opinions and experiences, they influence each other's purchasing plans.

Word-of-mouth is literally as old as the world itself. If you look at the results of this research, they confirm our original statement that people have had an impact on each other's buying behaviour since time immemorial. This social phenomenon still exists today, and it is in this sense that we assert that consumers, in essence, have not really changed all that much throughout the years.

The informative web, the social web, the semantic web, the... web

So has nothing changed in comparison with the previous century? Of course it has! The consumers of today have the internet at their disposal, a powerful medium that links them directly to the big, wide world. During the last three years the internet has reached the tipping point of its success. A large part of the world's population uses the internet daily. In 2010 there are more than a billion and a half users worldwide.[2] The average internet penetration in Europe, Oceania and the United States is 66 per cent. Since the year 2000 the number of surfers has quadrupled.

As time passes, so the online-behaviour of consumers also changes. At the opening of the 21st century the internet was little more than a place where you could find and read information: in other words, a digital information 'platform'. This information was primarily provided by companies, journalists and authors. Communication between the users of this information, the consumers, was then unusual. However, in recent years the informative web has been transformed into a social web. Everyone has become his or her own author. Reacting to articles, taking part in discussions and posting your own status updates on *Facebook* are just a few examples of the social experiences now available on the web. This social web now puts consumers in touch with each other. This development has had a major impact on the way the internet is used, and how consumers make their buying decisions. Because the internet allows everyone to have their own say, the amount of available information relating to product experience has increased dramatically. Consumers give each other feedback about products and brands – and this informa-tion influences the buying behaviour of their fellow surfers. Con-sumers use the information on the social web to reduce the level of risk associated with their purchases, or to find the lowest price, or to quickly find the right product information.[3] Consumers trust each other. Research has shown that 88 per cent of consumers have faith in their peers.[4] But the same consumers have much less trust for top-down communication. If a company manager puts out an information release, this is much less convincing than if the same information is spread by a member of staff or a customer of the company. In particular, this later channel of communication is re-garded as an objective, neutral source.

Conclusion: the social web puts consumers in contact with each other.

This has resulted in a change of behaviour on the web. People have become the authors of all kinds of different information, including texts about brands and products. This information influences the buying behaviour and the brand preferences of consumers.

Do you have confidence in the under-mentioned people?

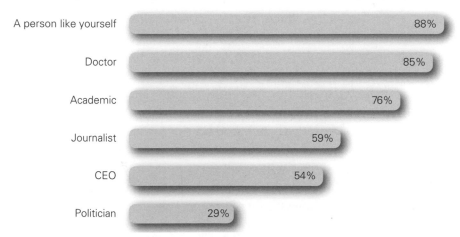

A person like yourself	88%
Doctor	85%
Academic	76%
Journalist	59%
CEO	54%
Politician	29%

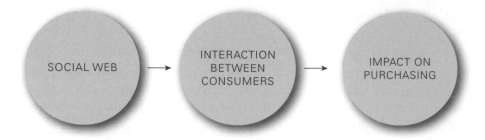

However, the social web by no means represents the end of digital evolution. The next stage is likely to be the semantic web. Whereas the social web links people to each other, the semantic web will link knowledge.[5] The semantic web interprets questions from consumers. The web becomes 'intelligent' on the basis of the information available to it. It will be able to separate relevant information from the irrelevant.[6] This means that consumers will be able to seek more accurate information about particular brands. As a result, the importance of online-information in relation to buying behaviour can only increase.

But the semantic web is only another step on the path to the ultimate digital experience: a fully integrated digital world. By 2020 the technology will be available to link intelligence.[7] The classic example is of a fridge which tells you when you need to buy milk. In this vision of the future our physical environment will become increasingly 'endowed' with intelligence, so becoming part of a larger network.

Machines will collect data from the physical world and will post it straight onto the web:[8] GPS sensors and security cameras are examples of equipment which already possess this capability. In the future your GPS will probably be able to tell you that you are late for your appointment, thanks to its link to your online agenda. It will then offer you the possibility to phone your appointment to tell them your new expected arrival time, using built-in real-time traffic information. This is the ultimate combination of online and offline information. Purchases will be based on the context-related information which the consumer will automatically receive. And the digital context of the consumer will result in targeted and accurate buying advice. This evolution will turn the current relationship between advertisers and consumers on its head.

Make your own diagnosis

The pharmaceutical industry is the ideal sector in which to examine the impact of the social web. Health care is a matter of great importance to almost every consumer – and hence it is an area to which he/she devotes a great deal of attention.

　If somebody becomes ill, they do not normally go straight to a doctor. The reaction of most consumers is to turn first to the internet, to see if they can find out something more about their symptoms.[9] What have I got? How serious is it? What are my options? These are all natural questions for a consumer to have in these circumstances. And he uses his knowledge, obtained from the internet, to formulate his own initial answers. Once he has formulated his hypothesis, a discussion process begins. He talks to his family and friends, or he logs on to one of the special portal sites dealing with health matters. Only then will he finally think about visiting his doctor in order to agree a final diagnosis and possible treatment. In fact, nowadays 10% of 'patients' make their own decision about the type of treatment and medicine which they want their doctor to prescribe for them.[10]

Oprah is dead!

On 20 September 2008 the following bulletin was posted on an American news website:

> Oprah Winfrey, aged 54, was discovered dead this morning on the floor of her house in Chicago. The local police and the FBI have imposed a news blackout. The first unofficial reports tell how Oprah was found with a wound in the vicinity of her eye, a bullet wound in the stomach and various stab wounds.

Within minutes several websites had copied this announcement. The news spread like wildfire on sites such as CNN and BBC *World*. A short time later, there were already rumours that the news had been confirmed in a news broadcast on American television. Hundreds of people began writing obituary messages on websites all over the world. Almost everyone who heard the news was profoundly affected by it.

　It was only hours later that it became clear that the whole thing was a set-up. A number of internet users wanted to demonstrate the power of the medium in a negative manner to the world. And boy did they

---

Social Search is taking over

In 2011 consumers will be more inclined to seek information via *Social Search* than through traditional search engines, such as *Google*.[11] In contrast to its 'rivals', *Social Search* does not trawl the entire internet for information. It only searches for information linked to relevant persons: friends on *Facebook*, contacts on *LinkedIn* and *Twitter*, people with a similar online profile, and so on. People looking to find a good restaurant for Saturday night are much more interested in hearing the opinions of their friends than the impersonal opinions dished up via *Google*. *Social Search* also offers the possibility to ask questions during the search process. This brings a whole new dimension to online enquiries.[12]

---

succeed! The dozens of news sites which had already posted the bulletin as 'breaking news' quickly and quietly removed it, and there was very little follow up to the incident: no reports and no prosecutions.

This story is an example of the kind of impact which the modern consumer can have. Consumers use the power of the social web to tell stories in a believable way to a waiting public. The story about Oprah was a complete fabrication. However, the vast majority of consumers write about their authentic experiences in the hope of helping other consumers in the same position. The consumer therefore has a powerful medium at his disposal to communicate with others on a grand scale.

The consumer has the world at his fingertips

The internet is the largest facilitator of word-of-mouth communication in the history of the world. Before the birth of the internet, the false announcement about Oprah would have been nothing more than a good (or rather bad) joke in a youth group or a sports club. But in 2008 it was able to create a furore around half the planet. Same announcement, different outcome.

The Word Of Mouth Marketing Organisation defines word-of-mouth marketing as follows: consumers who give information to other consumers about products and brands.[13] Word-of-mouth has two components: online and offline. The vast majority of word-of-mouth is still offline.[14] Having said this, online word-of-mouth reaches far more people than a traditional conversation. Both are important in the decision-making processes of consumers. More than half the information gathered by consumers during the decision-making process does not originate from the manufacturer.[15]

Both online and offline, people go in search of other people with similar interests and experiences, or the opinions of friends, or the advice and recommendations of independent professionals. Through this process of inter-communication consumers are able to influence each other.

Are you a member of Facebook?

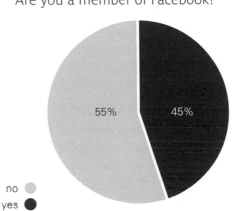

Forty-five per cent of Europe's internet users also belong to *Facebook*,[16] the largest social network site in the world. *Facebook* can be used to post messages and information about yourself, and to read similar messages and information from others. It is a new (and very effective) way to keep in contact with an extensive circle of friends. In addition, people link themselves explicitly to particular brands on this site. Consumers talk about their experiences. They make comments about products and services, and share them with their friends. Thirty per cent of the visitors from fora and discussion groups are deliberately searching for users of specific brands.[17] Asking questions and receiving answers about these different brands via online fora is now a reality on the social web.

Word-of-mouth has always existed, but it has gone into overdrive during the social phase of development which the internet is currently undergoing. This social phase has enhanced and intensified certain consumer characteristics. This has resulted in the creation of the four dimensions which typify the modern consumer:[18]

- **The consumer is a post-modern nomad**
  Online and offline are not two different worlds. In their mind's eye, marketeers see two completely different people if they imagine the internet user and a visitor to a shop. It is about time that they realized that we are talking about one and the same person.

- **The consumer uses his impact**
  Everyone is linked to the web and therefore possesses a tool which allows him to share his brand experiences better with others. There is a growing awareness of the 'power' which exists between consumers.

- **The consumer shows his emotion**
  Decisions are taken on the basis of a combination of rational and emotional aspects. The internet has heightened the emotional content of this process. Explicitly sharing your emotions with a larger group of people is a new trend.

- **The consumer is a part-time marketeer**
  Because of the greater availability of information, the world is becoming more transparent than ever before. Marketing is

The added value of the internet

The statistics which prove the added value of the internet to consumers are impressive, almost mind-bogglingly so. By the middle of 2010:[19]

- Every minute 20 hours of film are being loaded onto YouTube.
- You would need 1,412 years to watch all the films currently on YouTube.
- There are 133 million blogs in the world.
- There are 900,000 blog messages written every day.
- There are 50 billion Twitter messages written every day.
- 3,500,000 people follow Obama on Twitter.
- There are 400 million active users of Facebook.
- Each month 3 billion photos are loaded onto Facebook.
- Wikipedia had 684 million visitors in 2008.
- Google processes 2 billion search tasks each day.

You can get an update of these figures via the video 'Conversation Revolution', which you can find on YouTube.

now a subject in which each consumer has personal expertise. This new skill is something that they enjoy playing with.

The consumer is a post-modern nomad

The consumer demonstrates his post-modernism by the smooth and efficient manner in which he combines the online and offline worlds. Marketeers are inclined to see two different people when they think of an internet user and a consumer. But a consumer is a consumer. And he is now also a consumer of the internet. Internet plays an important part in the life of the modern consumer, but he is still the same person. Ninety per cent of people behave in exactly the same way online and offline. There is only a small minority which 'dares' to play another role during their surfing sessions.[20] People have the talent to choose the best channels for both their communication and their information searches. Nowadays, arranging a night out with your friends is a piece of cake via a social network. The days when you had to telephone your friends one by one to agree a fixed time and place are long gone. In fact, they belong to another century...

The arrival of the internet on the one hand and the development of cheap mass transportation on the other hand mean that the consumer is now free to discover the world. The consumer is a nomad, wandering in search of new information and new experiences. The expression 'the world is a village' could have been coined with the 21st century in mind. It is the perfect motto for the new digital era. The consumer now finds himself in a small and ever-shrinking world. Ten years ago, the best restaurants were largely visited by diners from the surrounding region. Now people fly half way around the globe to dine at El Bulli, the best restaurant in the world. Information is much more accessible to the average consumer than it was a decade ago. Consumers explore the world, both physically and digitally. During these voyages of discovery they are exposed to countless different messages which enrich their personalities. However, their wanderings also mean that consumers are required to process much more advertising material than ever before. As a result, our post-modern nomad has become more selective with regard to commercial messages.

Several years ago Seth Godin wrote that advertisers should regard the attention which they are given by consumers as a precious gift, and not as something to be expected, almost as a right.[21] An American consumer is bombarded with a staggering 3,000 advertisements each day.[22] It is impossible for one person to process so much information, and so they go in search of other, easier sources of information: other people. Moreover, they also go in search of more targeted information. In future, *Social Search* (see box, page 8) will increase in importance. Information derived from the consumer's personal network is often the most relevant information. This allows a greater degree of confidence when taking those important buying decisions. Increased social pressure also results in an increase in 'extreme' attitudes towards brands. Friends encourage each other to change washing powder, toothpaste, etc, particularly if someone in your network has had a bad experience with a product. Consumers soon find an alternative if their favourite brand lets them down. The effort required to move from brand A to brand B has never been so low. On the other side of the coin, the opposite is also true: the social web allows popular brands to increase their number of 'fans'. People share their positive feelings when their identification with a particular brand grows. In short, both these scenarios are possible.

Joseph Jaffe[23] has described it very well: brands must copy the behaviour of top tennis players. They see every point as crucial. The real champion can withstand the pressure of being love-forty and three match-points down, and can still fight back to win. Advertisers will only be able to increase customer loyalty if they regard every contact with their consumers as a 'now-or-never' moment.

The consumer uses his impact

The consumer has become more influential with regard to brands and advertising. We all have the means at our disposal 24/7 to launch messages into the world about anything we like or dislike, including brands. What used to be the exclusive privilege of the mass media (radio, television, newspapers) is now within the reach of everyone. E-mails, texts on fora, messages on *Facebook* and film clips on *YouTube* are the most important channels to get your ideas and opinions across. When *Time Magazine* chose 'You' as its Person of the

Year for 2006, this was simply a reflection of the media power that we all now have at our fingertips. In the 21st century, every person is a medium.

This media power has been made possible by the greater connectivity of our society. At home, at work and at many other places as well, consumers are in contact with each other via the web. The arrival of mobile networks has given the consumer the possibility to be continually online. Connection with the internet is much more than just a simple technological fact; it is also a social phenomenon. People are now connected with their family and friends. This means that the consumer is always able to get quick and personally relevant answers to all his questions, no matter where he is and no matter what the hour. He is also able to answer the questions of others and to post whatever message he pleases online. But that is not all. Lots of people now have a mobile phone with a camera function. This allows them to clarify and illustrate their brand experience with videos and photographs. I must confess that this is something that I am also 'guilty' of: I regularly use my cell phone to share my positive and negative experiences with my network via *Facebook*. Recently, I became irritated at having to wait too long at the check-out of a relatively small supermarket. Almost before I knew it, all my friends could read about my ill temper on my *Facebook* page!

Consumers are all too well aware of their new status and their new potential. This leads to a certain urge to express themselves. Each day, millions of people are telling the rest of the world about their daily lives and activities, their hopes and fears, their likes and dislikes. The internet is being flooded by 'content' generated by consumers. Why do people do this? Fifty-nine per cent claim that they like to share their knowledge with others; 30 per cent want to express themselves in a creative manner; and 17 per cent want to strengthen their personal image.[24]

The consumer has a strong impact on the society in which he lives, thanks to the mutually strengthening interplay of three distinct phenomena: everyone is a medium, everyone is connected, and everyone's need for self-expression is increasing. Later, we will see that a traditional advertiser regards these trends as some kind of threat. The loss of full control over the brand process makes him insecure. In contrast, the Conversation Manager will encourage these trends. He regards the influential consumer as a valuable sparring partner in the build-up of a brand.

Michael Jackson immobilizes the internet

Michael Jackson died on 25 June 2009. The world lost one of its most popular icons and the news caused an unprecedented storm of activity on the internet. The first announcement about Michael Jackson's death appeared on the showbiz site, *TMZ.com.* but the claim was not immediately confirmed by other news sources. Around the globe, distraught consumers sought more information about the pop star's death. Was it true? How did it happen? The massive surge of surfers caused the reaction time of the major new sites to drop from 4.2 seconds to 8.9 seconds.[25] *Google* even closed the page with search results for 'Michael Jackson' for several hours. The increase in the number of search tasks was equivalent to a large-scale internet attack. People turned to *Twitter* and other social network sites to try to find out what was going on. It was only later in the evening that the tragic news was officially confirmed. By midnight, nearly every *Twitter* message was related in some way to the death of the pop idol. Six per cent of all blog posts that day were linked to Michael Jackson. Only Obama scored better that day, with 8% – but it was the day of his inauguration as president.[26] The modern consumer was too quick for the world's fastest news agencies. As soon as the rumour appeared, the floodgates opened.

People make the news in Iran

When popular demonstrations broke out in Iran in June 2009 following the announcement of election results, the Iranian government tried to keep foreign journalists away from the worst affected regions. The only available information came from local Iranian people, who kept the world informed about their country's problems via their social networks. The Iranian regime blocked sites like *MySpace* and *Facebook*, but they were unable to shut down *Twitter*. *Twitter* is an open system, which means that you can update a profile via an sms. The photo-site *Flickr* also remained operative and was used widely. In just nine days, some 4,000 photographs of the demonstrations were uploaded. The power of the modern consumer – even in a country like Iran – allowed the world to follow the action as it happened.[27]

KFC loses 20 per cent of its value in just one week

A few years ago Kentucky Fried Chicken learnt the hard way about the negative side of modern consumer power. On 23 February 2007 a group of friends went to lunch in a Kentucky Fried Chicken restaurant in New York City. To their amazement, they saw a number of seemingly well-fed rats running around in the dining area. The shocked visitors reached for their mobile phones and began filming the spectacle. Not much later, the videos were being admired by tens of thousands of viewers on *YouTube*. The same evening, the pictures were broadcast during a CNN news programme.[28]

Moral: if something is wrong with your products or services in our contemporary society, the world will soon get to know about it. The consumer is appalled (and who can blame him) at rats running around in what is supposed to be a hygienic restaurant. And he now has the attitude and the means at his disposal to let his displeasure be known – to the world. And the consequences? Well, for KFC it was pretty disastrous. People considering a fast food meal on the day after the film was shown would probably think twice before risking KFC. 'Perhaps we'll try Burger King today.' Within a week of the rat video Kentucky Fried Chicken's stock-market quoting had plummeted by 20 per cent.[29]

This is a difficult situation for management to deal with. There are thousands of KFC restaurants around the world, but problems in only one. Yet the whole company was punished for this single rotten apple. As Jaffe said: 'Every contact with the customer is a now-or-never moment. Today's consumer has very little empathy with – let alone sympathy for – a company which disappoints him.' Mistakes and failures are more transparent than ever in our modern society – and therefore less acceptable than ever.

Wikipedia more correct than Britannica

A unique example of the behaviour of the post-modern nomad and the increasing impact of the consumer on society is the success story of *Wikipedia*.

Imagine if someone had said to you 15 years ago that an encyclopaedia would exist which everyone could consult free of charge, which contained fewer errors than the *Encyclopaedia Britannica* and which was compiled and maintained by a team of 75,000 volunteers. Would you have believed them? I very much doubt it. But today that encyclopaedia has become a reality.

Each year 684 million visitors enjoy the free information provided by the *Wikipedia* site. And the success of *Wikipedia* stands in sharp contrast to the decline of the once-respected *Encyclopaedia Britannica*. *Wikipedia* has literally a thousand times more visitors than *Britannica*, which is finding it hard to stay afloat.[30]

Many people still have difficulty believing that an encyclopaedia put together by 'ordinary' consumers can offer the same level of quality as the company which for decades has been seen as the standard bearer in the sector. And yet it is true. The science magazine *Nature*[31] carried out a random survey of 50 articles from *Wikipedia* and 50 from the *Encyclopaedia Britannica*. When the survey was first conducted, there were 162 errors in *Wikipedia* as opposed to just 123 in the *Britannica*. However, in a subsequent test a number of weeks later the researchers noted that the number of errors in *Wikipedia* had fallen, whereas the number in the *Britannica* remained more or less the same. Thanks to its correction processes, *Wikipedia* was evolving, but the *Britannica* was standing still. In June 2008 the *Britannica* management announced the launch of a collaborative 'platform' to develop its content. In other words, they decided to copy *Wikipedia*. But the chances of success are slim. Consumers are not likely to be motivated to build a second *Wikipedia*.

Wikipedia is one of the strongest proofs of the power of the modern consumer. By working with others, the consumer is capable of achieving a level of knowledge which it is impossible for an individual (ie an expert) to reach.[32]

Goggles offers protection against powerful emotions

We have all done it. In an impulsive moment of anger or frustration we send off an e-mail that was more harshly-worded than perhaps we really intended. A few minutes later, our anger is already giving way to remorse. But the damage has been done. The e-mail is already winging its way through cyberspace.

Google wants to protect consumers against their own emotions. To do this, they have developed a tool called 'Goggles'. If you install this tool, you first have to complete a few simple sums before you can send your mail. It is rather like the digital equivalent of counting to ten. But it gives you time to think twice before you hit the send button with your angry mail.

The consumer shows his emotions

Consumers take decisions on the basis of their emotions. The first scientifically accepted evidence for this truth was offered only as recently as 2002 in the book *Emotionomics*.[33] Viewed from a purely rational perspective, it makes more sense to buy a good quality shirt without a logo for 45 euros, rather than purchase a shirt with a Ralph Lauren logo for twice the price. Yet a significant number of people still opt for Ralph Lauren. Why? Emotionality – an emotional response towards the brand – is one of the explanations. In his recent book *Buy-ology* Martin Lindstrom has looked more closely at this phenomenon.[34] He conducted an experiment which registered brain activity when people were asked to look at the logos of different brands. Some of these brands (such as Apple, Ferrari, Harley Davidson and Guinness) excited more activity than other brands (including Microsoft). And the parts of the brain which were most stimulated were the parts dealing with memory, emotion and decision-making.

Since the scientific proof provided by *Emotionomics*, few people would dispute that consumers are emotional. My hypothesis is that consumers have always been emotional. However, in recent decades advertisers have tried to transform them into rational creatures, whose behaviour can be perfectly studied and explained.

In addition to implicit emotional behaviour, there is also explicit emotional behaviour: for example, the emotions which are explicitly shared with others via the internet. Forty per cent of *Facebook* users adjust their status at least once a week.[35] Each month there are 4 billion status updates. That is an average of 20 per month per user.[36] A status update is an expression of emotion. Comments such as: 'I can't really be bothered today' or 'I feel great now the sun is shining' or 'I hope the kids finally sleep tonight' are all examples of a change of emotional state. Sharing emotions is an enriching process for consumers. It offers them support and makes them feel better.

This phenomenon is particularly evident in the health sector, where the consumer's level of commitment is high. People who have just been diagnosed by a doctor nonetheless often return home uncertain and confused. At such moments, the patients are disappointed in the doctor's empathy (or lack of it). Today, this 'problem' can be solved by contacting fellow-sufferers on one of the many specialized discussion platforms. These sites not only offer moral support, but

A picture paints a thousand words

In 2006 Kodak launched a blog under the title 'A thousand words'.[37] This blog is a central element in the Kodak communication strategy. The content of the blog was spread via numerous social network sites (eg *Facebook, YouTube, Twitter*, etc). For Mother's Day, Kodak encouraged children to send 10 nice pictures to their website. For each picture, the children were also asked to choose an accompanying song. Kodak then made a stylish montage of the photos and the music and sent it back to the kids. It was an emo-gift – of the kind calculated to melt every mother's heart. But it was also a good example of how today's marketeers are trying to cash in on the latest trends in consumer behaviour.

are often a vital source of further information about the patient's illness and its consequences. Experiences which are shared in these fora can sometimes even lead to a change of therapy. As we have already stated: the sharing of emotions influences the decision-making processes of consumers.

Consumers also like to share their emotions with brands. In the run-up to Mother's Day, Senseo invited families to describe their

TUI links Tripadvisor to its international sites

TUI is a traditional travel agent, which for many years has been famous for offering package holidays to its many customers. In order to meet the changing expectations of the modern consumer, the company decided to add customer reviews to its website. But instead of building up its own review library, TUI decided to work together with Tripadvisor, one of the largest holiday review sites in the world. This meant that TUI consumers had access to a wide range of reviews right from the very first day. The collaboration also had the added advantage that the information was seen by consumers as being more impartial, which helped to increase the site's credibility.

---

mother's dream day on the Senseo website. More than 6,000 people took up the challenge and Senseo offered the writers of the best five entries the chance to turn this dream into reality. The other consumers were informed of the results in a special mailing to ensure that they did not feel forgotten. If a brand asks consumers for an emotional response, they very often get it.

Hug an M&M

Question: how do consumers express their emotions towards brands? Answer: in a hundred different ways. The supporters of a football team will wear a scarf in their team's colours. Harley fans will have

the Harley logo tattooed on their arm. Others may buy the same make of car, time after time. Others talk incessantly about how brilliant their new iPhone is, and are happy to demonstrate all the latest add-ons. Expressions of emotion of this kind are a golden opportunity for marketeers.

Some brands find it easier to stimulate consumer emotions than others. Brands such as Disney and the Leading Hotels of the World hardly need to do anything at all. The right atmosphere combined with a little light music, and the emotions come flooding out, all by themselves. But a brand such as M&M's doesn't have it quite so easy. How do you get emotional about a sweet? Nevertheless, M&M's has invested considerable resources in an attempt to develop a stronger emotional bond between their brand and their consumers. The first part of the strategy – and very effective it was, too – was to make the sweets come to life in their commercials as cartoon characters. This was the Disney philosophy applied to the confectionery industry – and it worked. The brand became more human and more personal, creating a greater degree of emotion amongst its target group. The company then went a step further by opening its own M&M stores. There are currently M&M stores in New York, Las Vegas, Orlando, Chicago and a number of other cities. The store in Las Vegas is three storeys high and is packed with M&M goodies and gadgets. And who do you meet when you enter the building? Who else – the M&M sweets, of course! You can shake hands with an M&M, be hugged by an M&M or even have your photo taken with an M&M. Cute, very cute. By turning the sweets into walking-talking beings and by attaching an experience to the brand, the level of emotional commitment was raised significantly.

The consumer is a part-time marketeer

In the old days, knowledge was the preserve of the marketeer, so that you could convince the consumer of more or less anything you wanted to. In contemporary society, this knowledge is now available to everyone. The modern consumer lives in a transparent world. With a click of his mouse he can find answers to even the most difficult questions. A quick search on *Google* or *Wikipedia* can work wonders. Many companies still have the arrogance to think that they can pull the wool over their consumer's eyes. Reality, however, suggests that sooner or later the truth will always come to light. Consumers have developed a kind of sixth sense, to sniff out the authenticity (or otherwise) of a marketing message.

This could be seen, for example, in a marketing campaign which Vichy (L'Oréal) launched a number of years ago. The campaign was designed to support a new anti-wrinkle cream that was being brought onto the market. As part of their total marketing strategy, the advertising agency decided to open a blog. A fictitious authoress, Claire, was the main character on the blog, and it was her role to pretend to be a real person. This turned out not to be such a good idea. After a few hours people soon caught on to the fact that the blog was a phoney, and Vichy felt obliged to apologize to the entire online community.[38]

Consumers are no longer prepared to accept it when companies try to pull a fast one. It is only by telling authentic stories that you will be able to win their trust.

Nowadays, consumers understand marketing actions far better than in the past, since they have become skilled in the marketing of their own personal positioning. In short, everybody is now an experience specialist. The so-called 'professional' experts claim that 'ordinary' people do not really understand what they are doing when they communicate online. But nothing could be further from the truth! They know perfectly well that they are writing on a public domain and they are clever enough to take account of this fact. Seventy-five per cent of *Facebook* users bear in mind that what they write can be read by others. Just 16 per cent are prepared to leave their personal details on social network sites.[39]

Strangely enough, consumers are also able to help marketeers and advertisers in their work. Fons Van Dyck[40] has already argued that the consumer is in reality a marketeer. You can – and should – involve him actively in your product development. He points to the example of Volvo, where women are used to help with the conceptualization of new car models.

Research carried out by InSites Consulting[41] suggests that consumers are open to the idea of collaborating with companies: 45 per cent would be happy to work on a new advertising campaign, 53 per cent would like to develop new products with the manufacturers and 66 per cent are keen to offer feedback about new products. The most important reason for this willingness to cooperate is intrinsic motivation. Financial inducements are less important to today's consumers. Moreover, this openness is to be found right across the board: at least 30 per cent of the consumers in each sector are ready to help in this manner.

Are you interested in...

45%
Taking part in a new advertising campaign

53%
Developing new products with the manufacturer

66%
Giving feedback about new products

Marketeers who still dare to underestimate today's consumers are taking a serious risk. Campaigns which try to mislead the public are almost certain to run into trouble. The biggest danger is that the world will very quickly realize what is going on. Bearing in mind the typical characteristics of the modern consumer which have already been mentioned, it is much better to adopt an open and authentic approach. The 21st-century consumer walks into the shop armed with a whole battery of knowledge, gleaned from his own trawling of the internet. All too often he is met by a salesperson who assumes that his customers know nothing. This can lead to embarrassing situations where the consumer actually knows more about the product he wants to buy than the shop assistant who is trying to sell it to him![42]

Dove: the making and breaking of a marketing campaign

The Dove brand (Unilever) has been trying to break through the 'classical' ideal of beauty in its advertisements. These efforts began following a research project entitled *The real truth about beauty* (2004). This study showed that large numbers of women were simply not prepared to take part in certain social activities because of their own negative self-image.[43] In particular, it was discovered that young girls have the lowest levels of self-esteem. The core conclusion of the final report was that '92 per cent of all the young girls in the world would like to change something about their appearance'. However, the report also suggested that mothers can play an important role in helping to develop a more positive image in their young daughters. On the basis of this research, Dove started the Dove Self Esteem Fund in 2005. At the same time, its 'Evolution' campaign was launched. This advert was viewed by more than 7 million people on *YouTube* and won all the major prizes at the advertising festival in Cannes in 2007. Through this campaign, Unilever wanted to reach mothers and encourage them to speak to their daughters about authentic beauty. 'The media is deceiving us all' was a clear message of their advertisement. The most telling image was when the face of a woman was reworked with Photoshop. Millions of people visited the 'Campaign for Real Beauty' website and supported its message by sending the *YouTube* clip around the world. Public reaction was full of praise and the brand value of Dove rose to levels significantly above those of it competitors.

Contemporary consumers were able to empathize fully with this campaign: the story brought an emotionally charged subject, which touched the lives of many, into the public arena. The message was believable and relevant (during this period there was a public outcry about a *Playboy* photo-shoot in which the navel of one of the models was air-brushed out with Photoshop).

A year later Dove launched a follow-up campaign entitled 'Onslaught'. This time, the style and approach of the advertisement was completely different, and slightly more aggressive. The message remained broadly the same: that the classical ideal of beauty was a burden for most young people, and that parents have an obligation to address this problem. One other aspect of the advertisement was different: the enemy was no longer the media – this time Unilever had its sights focused on the cosmetics industry. The campaign slogan was: 'Talk to your child before the beauty industry does.' The reactions to this new – and in many ways pioneering – campaign were mixed. In particular, 'only' half a million people watch the ad-clip on *YouTube*, and here and there a number of critical voices were raised. The relationship between Unilever, Dove and AXE was openly discussed on the *Contexts*[44] website. Some people were uncomfortable with the idea that AXE (another Unilever brand) used ultra-slim models in its campaign to sell male perfume – thereby perpetuating

---

The one million dollar page

The *milliondollarhomepage*.com is a case which perfectly demonstrates many of the facets of today's modern consumer.[45] It is the story of a clever and opportunistic consumer who came up with an irresistible pitch. In 2005, Alex Tew, an English student, started the *milliondollarhomepage* as a way to pay for his university studies. His home page was made up from a million pixels, and his business plan was to sell each pixel for one dollar. At one point, according to Alex, his website was the 126th most visited website in the world. On 1 January 2006 the last pixels were sold on *eBay* and his total turnover amounted to an amazing 1,037,000 dollars. This is an example that is impossible to repeat. It simply cannot be copied. Its success was largely attributable to its inherent authenticity: people 'believed' in the story.

---

precisely the type of stereotyped image that the Dove campaign was trying to break down. It had always been a risk choosing the beauty industry as a target, when Unilever was also a player in that same industry. It smacked of hypocrisy and the consumers began to ask some embarrassing questions.

The modern consumer: not just the most recent example of hype

'When will all that *Facebook* hysteria finally come to an end?' is a question that you often hear. 'At the end of the nineties we had the internet hype and in mid-2001 the bubble burst. Why should it be any different this time?' But these people are mistaken. The new consumer is a trend, not a hype. Moreover, it is a trend which changes the day-to-day life of all the consumers concerned.

The previous internet bubble had nothing to do with the use of the web. Instead, it had everything to do with the greed and the irrational behaviour of the financial markets. In those days, the bigger the loss you made, the more attractive your company became. This led to a price – earnings ratio of between 100 and 200, whereas the stock market average in 'normal' times is between 5 and 15. This over-valuation of the financial potential of the 'dotcom' companies was the real bubble, not the corresponding use of the web. The number of internet users actually rose during this period, and user intensity is still increasing. The average number of hours that people are active on the web each week rose from 5.5 hours in 2004 to 12.1 hours in 2008.[46] There is no question of the internet 'bubble' having burst.

In particular, since 2006 we have recorded a strong rise in the use of communities and social networking sites. This will continue to increase in the future. Metcalfe's Law states that the value of a network is equivalent to the number of its users squared (value = n^2). In concrete terms, this means that the greater the number of users in a network, the greater the value of that network and the greater its power of attraction for potential new users. It is an exponential curve.

This explains why it is difficult for the smaller social network sites to compete with *Facebook*. In view of the fact that 45 per cent of all Europeans are members of *Facebook*, the remaining 55 per cent who are perhaps thinking of joining a social network will first be attracted to the *Facebook* site, simply because so many of their friends will already be members.

What does this mean for marketeers and advertisers? The consumer clearly has more say than in the past. The four dimensions described above all have an impact on the manner in which consumers make their buying decisions. In the following chapter we will discuss their impact on the purchasing process in detail.

'Marktplaats' beats eBay[47]

The power of Metcalfe's Law is perfectly illustrated by the battle between *eBay* and *Marktplaats.nl*. In 1999 *Marktplaats.nl* was founded in The Netherlands as a site where consumers could sell all kinds of goods to each other – in short, a digital market place. This principle is the same as that used by the international giant *eBay*. At the start of the 21st century, *eBay* decided to embark on an expansion strategy. Local *eBay* offices were opened and almost every European land got its own national *eBay* site. This was also the case in The Netherlands, but the Dutch market proved to be one of the few markets in the world which *eBay* found it difficult to conquer. The reason for their defeat was simple: *Marktplaats.nl* was already very popular with the Dutch public. The number of registered buyers and sellers was high, so that the local value of the site was considerable. In the end, *eBay* decided that the only option was to buy *Marktplaats*. They paid 225 million euros, or 37.5 times the profit level. This was the only way to overcome Metcalfe's Law.

Everything online? The shop is king, and the internet its queen

Does the online evolution of recent years mean that the offline world has become unimportant to today's consumer? No, not a bit of it!

It is, of course, indisputable that online is increasing in importance, but the modern consumer needs a combination of both online and offline to determine his buying strategy. The search for information and the taking of the final buying decision both have a digital and a physical aspect.

Research by InSites Consulting has shown that nearly every consumer seeks information at the sales point (a travel agency, a bookshop, a supermarket). Different types of website will also be consulted: sites with consumer reviews, sites with expert reviews, comparison websites (eg *Kelkoo*). In fact, the consumer will make use of every available information source: brand sites, search engines, traditional advertisements or even documentaries on TV (for example, the holiday choice of many consumers is influenced by travel programmes). Moreover, consumers not only go in search of information, but are equally happy to provide it to others. After the processing of all this information, a final buying decision will be taken.

In most cases, this final decision is still made at the point of sale – the shop.[48] However, it would be wrong to infer from this that this is the most important place to commit your marketing resources. It goes without saying that some resources must be allocated to the point of sale, but it is equally (if not more) important to ensure that the consumer actually makes it to there in the first place. During the search for information and the discussions which take place between consumers on the internet, it is probable that some brands will already be discounted – and if your brand is one of them, then all your point of sale marketing is just so much money down the drain. It is therefore important to keep your brand in the running, so that the consumer still regards it as an option when they get to the point of sale – where they will make their final decision.

Hence our conclusion: the shop is still king when it comes to buying decisions, but the internet is indisputably its queen.

THE KEY POINTS IN THIS CHAPTER

- The internet facilitates word-of-mouth. The web has evolved from an information platform into a social tool. Consumers exchange information and affect each other's behaviour. In the years ahead, the influence of the internet will increase, as a result of further technological improvements.
- The modern consumer has a greater impact on brands than in the past. There are numerous examples of consumers making or breaking a particular brand. The arrival of the internet has enhanced certain aspects of the consumer's behaviour. Via the net, consumers can now communicate quickly and flexibly with other consumers and companies. In particular, the development of the internet has had an influence on four key aspects of the consumer's profile. Similarly, four key dimensions also have an influence on the manner in which advertisers now communicate with consumers.
- The consumer is a *post-modern nomad*: he understands the need and has the ability to combine the online and offline worlds. Both the physical world and the digital world are within his reach. This evolution has increased media pressure on the consumer, which makes him more selective when it comes to accepting (or rejecting) a particular marketing message. He trusts himself to find the information he needs and to make his own decision.
- Nowadays, the consumer has a much *greater impact*: every person is a medium. People are in almost permanent contact with each other via the web. Every consumer has the means and the ability to transmit his own 'messages' to the world and he can easily reach a wide network of people. Technological evolution allows the consumer to share his brand experiences with his family, friends and acquaintances both quickly and accurately. Information which would have been lost in the past is now digitally preserved 'for all time'.
- The consumer shows *emotion* – and these emotions are communicated more quickly than in the past. Using the internet, it is easy to find a group of like-minded people with whom you can share your emotions.

- The consumer is a *part-time marketeer*: promotions, advertising... the consumer fully understands the aims of all these marketing tools. Even more importantly, the consumer is a good marketeer of his personal identity. Using all different kinds of online tools, he succeeds in strengthening his own market positioning.
- Buying decisions are still normally taken at the point of sale: the shop. The internet is increasing in importance, but the offline environment is just as crucial. Consumers combine their online and offline worlds, and the marketeers will have to follow them.

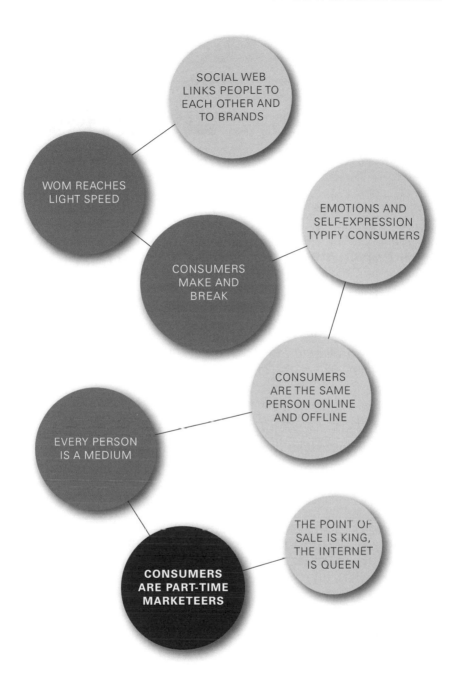

Chapter Two
The end of the 'traditional' advertiser

New consumers, traditional advertisers

Most marketeers were trained using the classic marketing works, such as those by Kotler. These theories worked perfectly in the days when the consumer was isolated from the world, allowing him to be easily manipulated by the media and the salespersons.

One of the central models in marketing policy is the AIDA model: Attention – Interest – Desire – Action. This is the flow through which the advertiser wishes to see the consumer progress. In order to sell a product, the consumer must first know that the product exists. Next, his interest can be aroused and his desire stimulated. A good marketing campaign contains a 'call-to-action', so that the consumer finally decides to buy the product. Communication plans and choice of media are largely determined by this strategy. But it is a strategy which results in the marketeer's message being rammed down the consumer's throat. Moreover, it is a strategy which requires a large media budget, to ensure that the number of consumers lost at each stage of the AIDA process is kept to an absolute minimum. More and more advertising is the most frequently used method to limit leakage from the AIDA funnel.

Unfortunately, this model takes little account of the characteristics of the modern consumer. A consumer takes his decisions on the basis of an investigative search in which he chooses his own preferred channels of communication. Discussions with other consumers help him to reduce his long-list to a short-list. And this is precisely the point where a number of brands leak from the funnel. In other words, it is now the consumer who has his hand on the tiller and is steering the ship – not the advertiser.

How does an advertiser try to relate to the new-style consumer? Occasionally, they will launch an action which takes account of his new profile. But few companies are prepared to fundamentally adjust their long-term marketing strategy. Soon or later, they return to the 'tried and tested' success formulas of the past.

Do you use the internet? (18–55 year-olds)

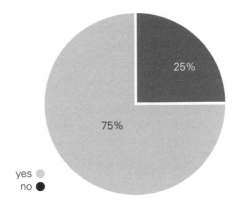

Even though the world has become a village for our post modern nomad, major companies are still organized on a regional basis for the implementation of their communication plans. For the 'Evolution' campaign Unilever had plans to stagger the release of this excellent advert in different lands. Local Unilever teams even considered making small adjustments to suit their own particular local markets. But what happened? When the film was launched, it had been circulated around the globe within days, by means beyond Unilever's control. Consumers do not think in terms of national boundaries. Advertisers do.

Advertisers are conscious of the growing impact of consumers, but fail to adjust their behaviour to reflect this fact. If I ask during workshops how many of the participants regularly check what consumers are saying about their brands online, the number of positive responses is surprisingly low. My personal estimate is less than 15 per cent. Yet these consumer comments are precisely the messages which steer the behaviour of other consumers! On *tripadvisor* I once discovered a photograph of someone who was showing their flea bites after staying the night in a particular hotel. My first reaction was: 'Who is going to want to stay at this hotel, having seen that photograph?' But this was quickly followed by a second reaction: 'I wonder if the owner of the hotel knows that this photo has been posted online?' We ignore the impact of the consumer at our peril.

Bring back the love

The Microsoft film *Bring back the love*[49] brilliantly highlights the contrast between the modern consumer and the traditional advertiser. If you have not seen the film, surf to *YouTube* and have a look at it now. It really is hilarious. The film shows a discussion between an advertiser (played by a typically slick man) and a consumer (played by a smart young woman). The pair are sitting in a cosy restaurant. But they soon begin to argue with each other. The consumer wants to break off the relationship with the advertiser, because she no longer feels understood. The advertiser reacts by saying that he understands perfectly who she is and what she wants: 'You are a woman, aged between 18 and 44 years, your hobbies are going out and playing sport, and you are interested in having laser-treatment to remove your leg-hair.' The advertiser does not understand that this has precisely the opposite effect on the consumer than he had intended. He even buys giant posters of her and puts them up in Times Square. As a last desperate measure, he showers her with savings vouchers and offers her the chance of winning a free trip to the Bahamas. If that doesn't prove his love for her, what will?

At no time during this amusing film does the advertiser ask his consumer a question. In fact, she can hardly get a word in edgeways. The ideas that he comes up with to woo her are all traditional marketing ploys. These all worked in the past, but now they are no longer enough to keep the smart consumer happy. Faced with such a lack of comprehension, she asks for a divorce.

A consumer shows his emotions. The expression and sharing of emotions with others via online channels has become a part of our modern-day way of life. For this reason, it is doubly disappointing that advertisers ignore this emotional side of the consumer's behaviour.

For example, the purchase of media time is a fairly abstract and reasoned process for most advertisers. Many of them seem to forget that they are actually buying time to tell their story to a potential customer. The advertiser views it all too coolly, too rationally. However, there are numerous opportunities for advertisers, if only they are prepared to make themselves more open to the consumer's emotions. Few brands offer consumers the chance to share their emotions and experiences. But if people are so anxious to tell their own stories about your brand, it is short-sighted not to play along with this situation – or even attempt to exploit it. Consumers are prepared to commit themselves to particular products on the basis of their emotional reactions.

ADVERTISER
ADVERTISER
Hey there, long time no see. You're looking good!
CONSUMER
Yeah ... let's keep things simple. I want a divorce.
We don't talk anymore!
I just put out a million on a TV commercial,
just to talk to you!
ADVERTISER
What about the print campaign? You can't tell me
you missed the billboard on Times Square?
You are saying you love me, but you're not behaving
like it. It's not genuine...
The agency said I was genuinely being funny.
They said you would love everything I did!
CONSUMER
Whether you are funny or not, I've changed and you
haven't. We don't hang out the same places anymore.
Sweetheart, I know everything about you! ...
I tell you what, come back here tomorrow and
I'll give you the chance to win a Bahamas vacation!

A tweet on Twitter can cost you 50,000 dollars[50]

In May 2009 a woman from Chicago posted the following message on *Twitter*. 'Just come and see me anyway. Who says that sleeping in a mouldy apartment is bad for you? Horizon thinks it's okay!' Horizon, a property group, failed to see the funny side of this message and promptly took the woman to court. They claimed damages of 50,000 dollars for defamation and potential loss of earnings. The message was initially sent to just 20 friends in the woman's network. But the key question is this: which approach would have been in the company's best interests? To slap a summons on the woman, or to talk with her about the things that were making her unhappy? Horizon went for the first option – but it turned out to be a bad choice. The original message might only have been sent to 20 people, but once it became news it was sent first to hundreds, and then to thousands. Before they knew it, a negative image of Horizon was being transmitted half way around the world.

Consumers are also capable of managing their personal brand through available online and offline channels. This allows them to understand and see through the strategies of the professional marketeers. They have become smarter than ever before – but few companies seem to realize this. There are many advertisers who would be well advised to show a bit more respect towards their consumers. Although they would never say it out loud, the majority feel themselves to be superior to the 'average' consumer. They send out mass consumption adverts on commercial stations, while they prefer to watch more informative programmes on other, more 'highbrow' channels. 'What's wrong with that?' you might ask. 'We are all different, aren't we?' Indeed we are, but as an advertiser it is difficult to understand the emotional reaction of the consumer to your advert, if you don't watch the programmes during which that advert is shown. This could tell you a great deal about your consumer's environment and mindset. Similarly, today's advertisers should not only buy the 'quality' newspapers, but should also read the popular press. This will help them to learn what is really going on in society, will give them new insights into the way people think and feel. These can be powerful weapons in the battle to win consumer loyalty. And the advertisers need all the help they can get. Consumers have changed out of all recognition during the past five years. During the same period the marketing industry has hardly changed at all.

Modern consumer	Traditional advertiser
Online and offline behaviour is the same	Online consumers differ from offline consumers
Are prepared to base decisions on the opinions of other consumers	Use traditional advertisements to persuade consumers
The world is a village without frontiers	Regionally organized
Gives continuous feedback on brands via word-of-mouth	Relies exclusively on traditional research to learn about the consumer
Lives surrounded by other consumers	Lives in an ivory tower
Emotional	Rational
Wants to converse	Can only shout

New consumers, traditional sellers

The new consumer not only has an impact on advertisers, but also on sellers. Sales staff who deal with consumers at the final point of sale will need to learn new sales techniques. Nowadays, consumers arrive in shops and stores armed with plenty of information about the products they want to buy. Just a few years ago, the majority of consumers knew very little when they entered a point of sale, and herein lies the biggest difference for today's salesmen and women: instead of passing on information to an ignorant customer, they now need to persuade customers who already have that information at their disposal.

During one of our marketing workshops, one of the participants told us the following tale. A few years ago he was thinking of buying a new BMW car, and so he visited one of the showrooms near his home. He had surfed the web in advance, and the details of the 'car configurator' were engraved in his memory. As a result, what he thought would be a pleasant experience – buying the car of his dreams – turned out to be a sad disappointment. He was interested in the 320d model, but with a reduced horsepower, so that the car would fall under a lower tax and insurance category. He had seen this idea mentioned on several of the websites he had visited and a number of his colleagues had suggested the same thing. However, during his visit to the showroom, the salesman seemed determined not to sell him that particular model. He even claimed that the model no longer existed, while the buyer was 100 per cent convinced that it did! After half an hour of not-too-friendly discussion, the potential customer left and immediately drove to another BMW distributor. This time he was told the truth. The salesman showed him the model he wanted and agreed that it was a smart buy: why pay all that extra money for extra horsepower that you can hardly ever use (unless you want to risk a speeding fine!). The customer placed his order the same day – with the second salesman, of course. The first seller had missed a good opportunity, as the man's company has since purchased a further 20 cars from the second distributor. The new consumer is not very forgiving if he is not taken seriously and will soon find an alternative solution of his own.

The second salesman was much smarter. He listened first to his customer's story and quickly realized that he was well informed – and so there was no point trying to pull the wool over his eyes with a well-rehearsed (and largely untrue) sales pitch. So he adjusted himself to the situation – and rightly so. If a consumer wants to buy a car, 60 per cent of them will have thoroughly investigated the website of their preferred make before ever setting foot in the showroom. Twenty-seven per cent will have sought additional material from other sites.

Sales people need to assess their consumers accurately. By asking a few well-targeted questions, it should quickly become apparent whether your consumer is well informed or not. There are still customers who arrive at the point of sale in a state of ignorance, but they are becoming few and far between.

Changed consumer: yes!
All-powerful consumer: no!

If the modern-day consumer now has such impact, what is the role of the modern-day advertiser? Has the consumer seized effective marketing power, so that the advertiser is reduced to a passive role on the sidelines? The answer to this question must be a resounding 'no!'

Who controls the conversations between consumers? The consumers? Or the marketeers? In Jaffe's opinion[51] nobody automatically has control. Everyone starts on the same level playing field. The password for advertising success in the coming decades is: *together*.

If everyone works together in the same direction, the results can often be impressive. For example, it is remarkable to witness how the Apple management team and Apple fans work together to further develop their chosen brand. If Apple announces a new product during a press conference, within hours thousands of Apple addicts are already spreading the message. The most fanatical Apple lovers even brainstorm about potential new ideas on the site *Macrumors.com*. In effect, these people pre-design new products for the Apple brand. They keep a watchful eye on patent offices to gain useful information for further product development.[52]

This example illustrates a simple but important message: together, advertisers and consumers are a powerful force. It is not a question of who has control; it is a question of working together in the best possible manner.

But there is also another question: will this kind of togetherness work for every brand? The answer is 'yes, but...' Yes, it will work, but only on condition that consumers identify fully with the brand. In some sectors brand commitment is easier to create than in others, but every brand has the potential to engage consumers in one way or another. However, the traditional techniques of the advertiser are insufficient to ensure the required levels of brand identification. Further in this book we will discuss how a Conversation Manager builds up his brand and gets his consumers involved.

Mass media have made us lazy

Since the arrival of mass media, the advertisers have had a tool at their disposal which allows them to send the same message to millions of people. These mass media have proven their value time and time again: brands such as Coca-Cola and Procter & Gamble became huge, thanks to their ability to communicate successfully through these media. However, in recent years these media have come under increasing pressure. As a result, the media have been subjected to a process of splintering. This in turn has meant that greater efforts are now required to maintain the impact level of advertisements. As long ago as 1997 an article

Fans build Coca-Cola on Facebook[53]

Coca-Cola is one of the most popular brands on *Facebook*. In total, Coke has more than 250 fan groups, and one of these groups has more than 3 million members. The group was not set up by Coca-Cola, but by the fans themselves. The page was launched by two friends, and it quickly became a big hit, without any real explanation why. Coca-Cola was also at a loss to explain its success. The most commonly cited reason was the quality and appeal of the photograph (a picture of a can of Coke). Another suggestion was that the founders had their own socially committed networks. But it continues to be largely a matter of guesswork.

The majority of companies react negatively to this kind of consumer initiative. When Coca-Cola first contacted the two fans, they were both worried that the company was planning to hit them with a law suit. But the Coca-Cola management had only the best of intentions. They invited the two young men to C-C headquarters in Atlanta to brainstorm about the future of the *Facebook* page. Coca-Cola didn't want to take over the page, but simply wished to exchange ideas with its creators.

appeared in the *Harvard Business Review*,[54] warning advertisers of the waning power of mass media: 'In the United States the mass media are the cornerstones of marketing policy. However, this norm is threatening to disappear. Fragmentation of the media and rising investment costs are already making things much more difficult. In the future there will no doubt be technological solutions which will allow individuals to deselect or bypass advertising altogether.'

The message is therefore simple: do not rely exclusively on mass media to build up your brand. Begin with a strong market identity and use your consumers to build on this identity. That was the message back in 1997, and it is still the message now.

The biggest advantage of mass media is their reach. But it is precisely this advantage which makes the advertisers lazy. By making an attractive advert (preferably in an exotic location) and by broadcasting it on popular commercial channels, the advertiser creates movement in the market without needing to do very much. A few days after the launch, the sales figures are examined and the short-term impact of the campaign is assessed.

The danger of this approach is that it encourages our advertiser to climb back into his ivory tower, where he discusses his further marketing strategy with his advertising agency and the media company. The advert is viewed on a large screen with perfect sound and image quality. The number of GRPs[55] will be discussed. At the end of the day, everyone has a good feeling. But the manner in which the advert has been viewed and assessed has very little in common with the way it will be viewed and assessed by the consumers. The consumer will see the advert sandwiched between his favourite programmes. His level of concentration will be lower than the advertiser's. In short, they will not be looking at the same thing. It is therefore the moral duty of every advertiser to climb back down from his ivory tower and join the rest of us – with our feet firmly on the ground. Advertisers must examine their own advertisements in their natural habitat: between the programmes shown on popular television channels. They must experience their adverts in the same way that their consumers experience them. This is the only way to gain a better understanding of those consumers.

The other disadvantage of the mass media is growing consumer resistance. Commercial pressure is increasing. Consumers realize that they are being asked to watch an awful lot of advertising. Faced with this increase in advertising pressure, the consumers are starting to put their foot down. They have had enough. In addition, the greater fragmentation of the media means that consumers are becoming harder and harder to reach. There are many more radio and television stations than there used to be, the number of magazines continues to grow, and, to cap it all, there are millions of internet pages which need to be taken into consideration. This fragmentation, combined with the emergence of a more self-aware consumer, is making it harder to play the trump cards of the mass media to maximum effect. For example, in 2006 it was necessary to broadcast an advert 150 times in order to reach 80 per cent of the American public. Back in 1987 the same effect could be achieved by just three showings.[56]

In addition, in recent years a number of other qualitative consumer trends have become visible which suggest that consumer resistance to advertising is growing. *Amazon.com* does a roaring trade in the sale of DVD boxes of popular television programmes. At first glance this might seem strange, since most of these programmes can be viewed free of charge on the commercial stations. And yet people continue to buy these boxes in large numbers. It seems that some consumers are not prepared to wait 24 weeks to discover how Jack Bauer will foil the terrorists this time. They want to know now; they want to decide for themselves when they watch and when they don't; and many of them want to watch without the interruption of adverts. And for all this, they are prepared to pay extra. Digital television is also causing the consumer to adopt a different approach towards advertising. The ability to wind on the advertisements is one of the most widely used features of digital TV.[57] The real interactive button is the fast-forward

Mickey Mouse goes porno!

On 12 October 2006 a new film appeared on *YouTube* which was not appreciated by the managers of the Disney Corporation. The film was actually made as a joke by several of the staff at Disneyland Paris, and showed a number of Disney figures having a good time. A very good time. In particular, there was a scene of Mickey and Minnie having sex with a snowman! The images were made just before the figures were due to take part in the Disney parade. The film was picked up by a number of the busiest newspaper websites and by the end of the day had been viewed by thousands of interested visitors. It created a major commotion: who would ever have believed such a thing of Mickey and Minnie?

The annual advertising budget of Disney is a staggering 1.8 billion dollars.[58] This is equivalent to 5 million dollars per day. Now ask yourself the following question: what is the consumer most likely to remember the day after? A sweet and innocent advert for Disneyland Paris? Or Mickey and Minnie humping the snowman? No contest. No matter how big your advertising budget is, the public always remember this kind of story much longer than any kind of traditional advertising material.

button! In other words, it is clear that it now requires much greater effort and much greater creativity to reach consumers through the mass media than it once used to.

And yet... the 30 second advert is not dead

The 30 second advert has been under fire for years. Figures show that it nowadays takes far greater resources to maintain the same level of impact as in the past. In other words, it costs more time and more money to reach the consumer using this traditional advertising tool. Even so... the 30 second advert is not yet dead. During the crisis of 2008–09, the management teams of various commercial channels announced the resurrection of the 30 second spot.[59] In these days of economic and financial insecurity, it seems that the advertisers are once again opting for 'certainty'.

Notwithstanding all the figures and reports which show that the consumer has reached saturation point with regard to televized advertising, a number of new studies have revealed more openness towards the 30 second spot. Sixty-five per cent of consumers expect that new brand products will be launched via the television.[60] Forty-four per cent would prefer to see this happen via the papers and just 40 per cent would prefer to learn about the launch via the web.

Through which channels should companies launch new products?

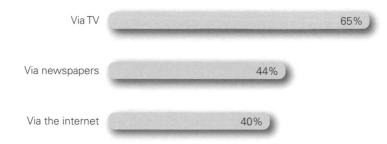

Via TV	65%
Via newspapers	44%
Via the internet	40%

Apart from the 30 second advert, the mass media continue to be crucially important for the strengthening of a word-of-mouth campaign. When Steve Jobs announced the launch of iPad during a press conference, it was immediately followed by significant levels of online buzz. But it was only once the news appeared in the papers and on the TV news that the real hype was born. To give added power to their new slogan 'Life's for sharing' T-Mobile launched a spectacular campaign, orchestrated by Saatchi and Saatchi. They organized a live event at one of London's major railway stations. It began with a single train passenger who began to dance in the middle of the station forecourt. A few seconds later, hundreds of other people were dancing to the beat of the infectious music. Dozens of real train passengers (the rest were all actors) also joined in. The object of the exercise was to create an event that people could share with each other through social media. And indeed, in view of the unique idea behind this stunt many people did send it on to their family and friends. A little later, the story of the film found its way onto television channels, radio stations and into the press. This led to a worldwide boost which resulted in the film eventually being seen by more than 17 million people. A real world hit. Even more importantly, the visibility created by the campaign was followed by a spectacular increase of 52 per cent in T-Mobile's sales figures.[61]

In most cases, word-of-mouth-communication needs the mass media in order to be successful. Research has shown that one in every five conversations about brands refers to an advert in a mass media channel.[62] The 30 second spots which make a real impact are the spots which contain striking or contentious elements. Give the consumer something to talk about, and they will happily spread your message. Word-of-mouth needs the mass media and vice versa. If the two come together, this acts as a catalyst which can shift your advertising campaign into overdrive.

Online advertising is different

During the early years of the internet explosion, the new medium was regarded as an extra channel of communication by the advertising experts. 'Banners' and 'skyscrapers' were bought and sold for dizzying prices. Just a few years later the buyers were left with a serious hangover. The really big advertisers had failed to find their way to the web and others had lost faith in the new medium as a viable advertising tool. At the time, these doubts were well founded, but only because the method of advertising was wrong. The advertisers treated the internet as though it was the same as every other mass media channel. Their approach was: 'we will compile our message, and the consumer will simply have to swallow it.'

However, the differences between television and the internet are enormous: TV is a 'lean-back' medium, where the consumer adopts a passive attitude; in contrast, the internet is a 'lean-forward' medium, where the consumer is pulling all the strings. This makes it necessary to develop a different kind of advertising for the internet. Advertising on the internet can only work if it takes proper account of the medium's strengths. The most important source of online advertising income is currently in 'search'. During the final quarter of 2008, 46 per cent of income came from 'search' activities.[63] 'Banners' are responsible for a further 21 per cent and small personal ads (eg job requests, second-hand trading, etc) for just 13 per cent.

Distribution of turnover for online advertising

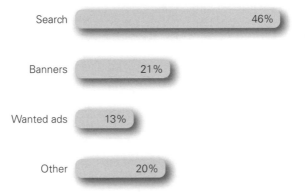

Search 46%

Banners 21%

Wanted ads 13%

Other 20%

Social advertising

Visionary advertisers are currently devoting a lot of their thinking to the concept of social advertising.[64] Social adverts are adverts which, with the prior permission of the consumer, include photographs of that consumer in the creative development process. This advert is then shown exclusively to the family and friends of that specific consumer. This means, for example, they may see a promotion for a new line of clothing, with their friend acting as a model. Social advertisements make use of the information which consumers share with their personal environment. What brands are important to them; what languages do they use; what kinds of photographs appeal to them: all these aspects are taken into account when creating these 'made-to-measure' spots. The social context of the consumer becomes the input for the personalized campaigns of the advertiser.

> ### Spain bans certain adverts before 10 o'clock in the evening
>
> Mass media continue to play an important and high-impact role in advertising. However, it is equally important that advertisers should have a Plan B up their sleeves – just in case. It is possible that in future it will become more difficult to reach consumers via the traditional mass media channels. A concrete example of the kind of problem which may arise recently occurred in Spain. In January 2010 the Spanish government banned all adverts for dietary or beauty products before 10 o'clock in the evening, because they were considered to be potentially dangerous. According to the government, there is a risk that such advertisements encourage a negative self-image, which in extreme cases may lead to 'inappropriate' cosmetic surgery. Conclusion: some sectors (including, for example, the tobacco industry) are forced to use alternative techniques to communicate with their target group.

The consumer is our partner: together we are strong

In 2000 one of the most visionary marketing books in recent years was published: *The Cluetrain Manifesto*.[65] The authors acknowledged that markets were going to change. In particular, they suggested that markets were going to get smarter, so much so that they will eventually be smarter than the companies. Markets (networks) are conversations. Markets are places where open, honest, direct, funny and sometimes shocking comments are made about brands. The human voice is authentic, and cannot be imitated. The knowhow of most companies consists in the repeated shouting of a single, monotone message to the market. It should therefore come as no surprise that the market will show little respect towards companies that demonstrate that they are unwilling or unable to converse in the manner that the market demands.

Consumers (markets) want to help companies. Half of Europe's consumers say that they are willing to work with the business community. They are prepared to help entrepreneurs to think about new products, new advertising campaigns or the improvement of customer service provision.[66]

Imagine that you are the manager of a sales force, with one hundred thousand staff to command... In these circumstances, you would expect your sales results to be rocketing off the scale. But the truth of the matter is that you already have a sales force of this size at your disposal – your consumers! All you need to do is activate them and then steer them gently in the right direction. Consumers are ready and willing to help – so don't forget it! Everyone dreams of brand loyalty like Apple. But don't kid yourself: this loyalty didn't simply materialize out of thin air. It had to be worked for – and worked hard. Twenty years ago Apple was almost bankrupt. Their current success is based on 20 years of consistent policy and open consultation with their consumers. Many of Apple's consumers are prepared to go through hell and high water for their favourite company – and in this way Apple is a perfect example of a company with a one hundred thousand-strong sales force.

The battle-cry of the 21st-century advertiser must therefore be: together we are strong! But the placing of the consumer on an equal footing requires a high degree of openness and courage. Lego believes strongly in this approach. A significant proportion of their new products are developed in collaboration with their consumers. In this way, Lego has built a consumer community of some 2.5 million people. In return, these people give Lego ideas about products. Concepts which are positively received by the community are earmarked for further development. The person who thought of the idea is granted 5 per cent of the royalties on the turnover of the product, once it is on the market. Perhaps not surprisingly, Lego receives between 3,000 and 6,000 new product concepts each week. Another subsidiary advantage of this platform is the fact that adults learn that there are plenty of other adults who are still interested in Lego. For a long time, many of these adults were afraid to admit their passion for a 'children's' toy, but in recent years adult participation in the platform has increased dramatically. The Lego philosophy can be summarized in the words of their own website: 'It's *not* about controlling our consumers, it's about *supporting* our consumers.'[67] Whether it is coincidence or not, Lego's turnover has increased by 20 per cent since the current economic crisis first began, while most other toy manufacturers have been having a much harder time.[68] 'Together we are strong.' It has certainly worked for Lego: it is largely the company's own customers who have come up with the most successful product innovations, to the benefit of all concerned. Talk about a win–win situation!

> ## Dunkin Donuts launches new products together with fans on Facebook[69]
>
> By working together with your fans, you can increase the visibility of a new product. Dunkin Donuts thought up a creative way to involve its *Facebook* fans in the launch of its new 'Coolatta' drinks. If you posted a photograph of yourself drinking a Coolatta as your profile photo on *Facebook*, you had the chance to win one of hundreds of great prizes. All 800,000 fans were invited to take part in the competition and each day Dunkin Donuts chose a number of winners at random. They each received a prize and their photograph was used as an icon on the Dunkin Donut fan-page.

Warning: the 1987 threat

The message is clear: the consumer has changed, but the advertiser has not – at least, not enough. The survival of the advertising industry in the 21st century will only be possible if advertisers conform more closely to the key trends in consumer evolution. One incentive to change is to ensure the continued success of your brand. But there are other, more important reasons. There is a new generation of advertisers in the making, a generation which has grown up in this world of conversations. For them, dealing with the new consumers is the most normal thing in the world. This generation forms a very real threat to your job.

People born in 1987 reached 21 years of age in 2008. After a three-year marketing course, some of them are already starting to work in our marketing companies. The more academically inclined graduated in 2009 and the postgraduates will be ready to hit the job market at the end of 2010. When this generation has acquired 10 to 15 years' experience, they will gradually ease today's marketing workforce to the sidelines. Why? Because the current marketing generation will no longer speak the right language. 'Tell me again what *Twitter* is?' 'What is the best way to say that on *Facebook*?' The new generation won't need to ask. They already know. They grew up with it.

There is a massive difference between the old and new generations of advertisers. Many of the older generation claim that they are open to the use of new methods of communication, and in 2009 some

80 per cent of them had the intention to launch a campaign on a social network.[70] However, only 30 per cent of these marketeers actually participate in a social network themselves (as opposed to 72 per cent of consumers). This is a disturbing finding. It is like expecting someone to advertise on TV when they have never even seen a television. Or like asking someone to advertise in a newspaper without knowing what type of paper is best to use.

The new generation of marketeers are the last wave of the Y generation.[71] They are 'digital natives'. They cannot imagine a life without a cellphone or the internet (because they have never known such a life), and they regard e-mail as outdated, outmoded and slow:[72] its only use (as far as they are concerned) is the transmission of large and bulky business documents. Social communication must provide instant feedback. Yet at the same time, they are also consumers of the more classical media. Eighty per cent of them watch at least half an hour's television every day and they spend at least the same amount of time surfing the net.[73] The majority of these young people use the world-wide web, mobile telecommunications and their MP3-player all day long – both before, during and after school. Multi-tasking and the urge to make maximum use of all available communication channels are built into their genes.

The generation born after 1987 has no difficulty in understanding the modern consumer. In fact, they are a reflection of that consumer: they have been combining online and offline activities in all facets of their lives, almost since the day they were born. They have the skills to communicate quickly and effectively. They understand the effect they have on companies and on each other. They are the inventors of status updates and the sharing of emotions via digital networks. Above all, they are experienced advertisers. Even before they arrive on the labour market, they have had years of experience at managing their own personal brand. Deciding what information to post on *Facebook* (and what not) is a part of their lives. Deciding which emotions (read: messages) they share with which people (read: target group) is an inborn natural talent.

Therefore I would launch this appeal: young people born in or after 1987, the marketing world needs you! Marketing is about understanding consumers and working together with them to achieve great things. Without actually knowing it, this is something that you could be really good at.

The challenge: surviving the conversation revolution

We live in fascinating times. With the possible exception of the industrial revolution, we are living in one of the greatest eras of human change in history. In the years to come, this period will be referred to as the conversation revolution. And a revolution inevitably means change. And change is something that many people have difficulty in accepting. As the inventor Charles Kettering once said: 'People are very open-minded for new things, as long as they are exactly like the old ones.' Change demands courage, openness and effort.

Today, for the first time in the history of marketing, we do not have the luxury of refusing to follow suit. The consumer has chosen resolutely to embrace the trends of the new revolution. As a result, consumer attitudes and consumer behaviour have been transformed in recent years. And so for the rest of us, there is only one remaining option: change as well – or go under.

Advertisers who succeed in understanding and managing the conversations between their brand and their consumers will be able to ensure the success of their products far into the future. Conversing with their consumers about their brands is their ultimate objective. The rest of this book will tell you the best way to approach this change trajectory. Think of it as a guide for your personal process of metamorphosis.

In order to make this process of change complete, we will now say farewell to the word 'advertiser'. An advertiser is someone who compiles messages, which he then shouts at the consumer. In the previous chapter, we have shown that shouting at someone is not the best way to convince them of anything. The best way to convince someone is by talking to them as part of a dialogue, by engaging them in conversation. Hence, from now on we will no longer be referring to advertisers, but will be using our new term: the Conversation Manager.

A Conversation Manager is someone who can listen to and talk with consumers. A Conversation Manager communicates with consumers, rather than at them. A Conversation Manager lives in and experiences the same world as the consumer. He can manage the new communication channels and techniques of the 21st century. In contrast to the advertiser, he does not ask himself what the central message of his new campaign should be. Instead, he looks for subjects that he can explore with his consumers. He helps the consumer to talk constructively about his brand.

If you want to keep one step ahead of the 1987 generation, there is only one thing that can save you: you have to become a Conversation Manager. By linking your experience to a number of crucial new insights, you can bring a new drive and determination to your daily job and give your future career a firm push in the right direction. Good luck with your change process. The advertiser is dead, long live the Conversation Manager!

THE KEY POINTS IN THIS CHAPTER

- The first chapter described the evolution of the modern consumer. It is strange that so many advertisers are aware of this evolution, yet have done so little to adjust their own behaviour and attitudes to reflect the resulting transformation in consumer behaviour. The consumer has changed, but *the majority of advertisers continue to bombard them with the same, old, traditional messages of the past.*

- The new decision-making processes of the consumer demand a new sales strategy. Salespersons continue to cling to their traditional techniques, whereby they wrongly assume that the consumers are ill-informed when they enter the point of sale.

- *Mass media makes advertisers lazy.* This has led to the creation of a gap between the world experienced by the consumer and the world experienced by the advertiser. Consumers are processed as GRPs, and are reduced to impersonal statistics, almost as if they are not really people at all. *The advertiser must get to know the consumer better – before it is too late.* Even so, mass media are by no means dead and buried. On the contrary, they play an important role in strengthening word-of-mouth messages.

- Advertising on the internet cannot in any way be compared with traditional advertising. Internet is a 'lean-forward' medium, where the consumer is pulling all the strings.

- The consumer *has more impact, but this does not mean that he is all-powerful.* Advertisers continue to play an important part in determining market strategies and tactics. The consumer has clearly risen in the advertising hierarchy and can now play an interesting new role. *Building brands together with the consumer is the major advertising challenge of the future.*

- *A new generation of advertisers has been born since 1987.* This generation of *web natives* has never known a life without the internet. Since the end of 2008, this generation has started to infiltrate the marketing industry and they form a threat to the existing generation of traditional marketeers. If these traditional marketeers want to survive in their chosen profession, they will need to change their attitudes and behaviour. *They will need to become Conversation Managers.*

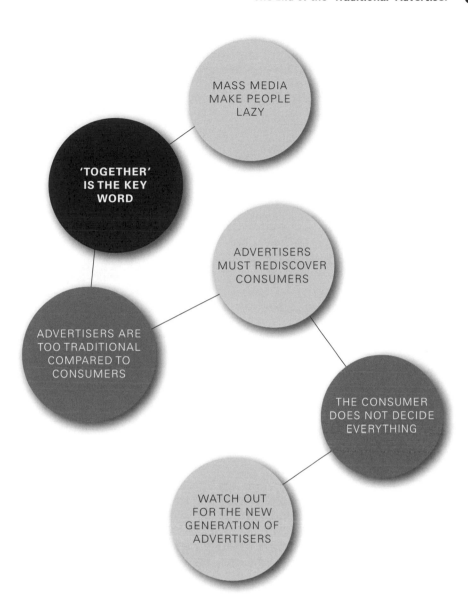

Part Two
The Conversation Manager

PART TWO CONTENTS

Chapter Three
The new framework

Before we start: shattering a few myths

In recent years I have given numerous workshops and presentations about Conversation Management. Some of my listeners find my story interesting, but irrelevant. The reasons for their scepticism are to be found in their own situation. They think that my story is not applicable to their particular sector. For this reason, I would first like to shatter a few of the more common myths about Conversation Management.

First myth: only online conversations are important

This myth can sometimes cause B2B-companies (business-to-business) to back away from Conversation Management. 'We only have a limited number of customers, so there won't be many online conversations about our company.' If your company only has between 20 and 200 customers, then it is probably true that there is little chance that they will communicate with each other online about your brand. But for this reason there is a much greater than average chance that they will talk about your products offline. The power of a personal recommendation is just as strong in B2B-companies as it is in B2C-companies *(business-to-consumer)*. In view of the high level of commitment involved in B2B decisions, the impact of these recommendations is correspondingly high. However, even with companies selling consumer products the majority of conversations still take place offline. Numerous studies[74] have confirmed that between 80 per cent and 90 per cent of all conversations about brands fall into this category.

These results actually encourage some of my listeners to turn the arguments on their head. They regard online conversations as being

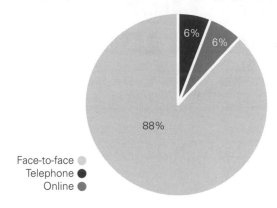

The majority of conversations take place offline

6%

6%

88%

Face-to-face ⬤
Telephone ⬤
Online ⬤

less valuable than their offline conversations. This is false reasoning, just as it would be equally short-sighted to ignore the impact of offline conversations. The volume of online conversations may be lower, but their reach is correspondingly greater. An offline conversation about a brand will probably involve no more than five people, while an online conversation can be followed by thousands. Moreover, the online conversation will be available for more or less permanent consultation on the web, whereas offline word-of-mouth is quickly forgotten.

A good example of the value of both online and offline conversations occurred in the aftermath of two press conferences held in January 2010. At the end of January President Obama gave his State of the Union address and during the same week Apple broke the news about the launch of the iPad. Research has shown that there was more online word-of-mouth about iPad than about the president's speech. However, the tone of the conversations was more positive for Obama than for Apple. At first glance, it may seem strange that there was more online buzz about a new piece of technology (however clever) than about the future of the American nation, but this is where the importance of offline conversations comes into its own. The offline word-of-mouth about Obama's speech was immeasurably bigger than the iPad's. In other words, both channels are important to get a total picture of what consumers are saying about your brand.[75]

During the past week, have you talked about...

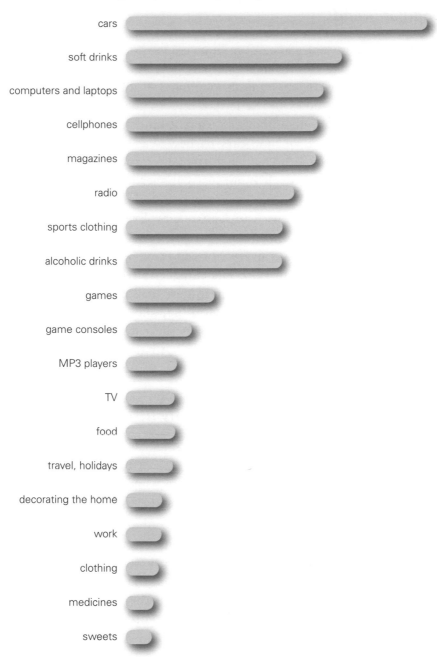

- cars
- soft drinks
- computers and laptops
- cellphones
- magazines
- radio
- sports clothing
- alcoholic drinks
- games
- game consoles
- MP3 players
- TV
- food
- travel, holidays
- decorating the home
- work
- clothing
- medicines
- sweets

Second myth: there are only conversations about popular brands

In Belgium there are some 25 million conversations about brands each week. In The Netherlands there are 37 million.[76] In the United States, the volume rises to a mind-boggling 3.4 billion conversations per week.[77] The studies by KellerFay and InSites Consulting have revealed that people talk about all different kinds of products nearly every day, ranging from new cars to new washing powders. This effect is heightened by the fact that almost every type of consumer likes to talk about brands. It is not just younger people who actively follow brands on the web. No, it is young and old, men and women, opinion-formers and mainstream consumers. Everyone talks about brands.

Yet although there are conversations in every sector, the intensity of these conversations can vary. The categories which are most discussed include cars, soft drinks, computers, cellphones, magazines, radio, alcoholic beverages, sports clothing, shoes and games. The fewest conversations are to be found in the categories for sweets, biscuits, clothing and home decoration.[78] All the other sectors fall somewhere in between.

Third myth: conversations are mostly negative

Many managers are afraid of conversations. They fear that their brand will be reviewed negatively in customer fora. This fear arises from research which has shown that dissatisfied consumers are more likely to share their opinions than satisfied ones.[79] On the other side of the coin, most companies have far more happy than unhappy customers. On average across all sectors at least 50 per cent of people express themselves to be very satisfied with their suppliers. Only between 6 per cent (cars) and 18 per cent (banks) report that they are dissatisfied.[80]

Look at your own situation. Consider all the things you use at home and at work, and ask yourself whether you are generally satisfied with their quality and performance. In most cases the answer will be 'yes', for a more limited number your feelings will be neutral, and only for a very small minority will you be actively hostile.

Conclusion: although people are more ready to share their dissatisfaction than their approval, the balance in brand conversations

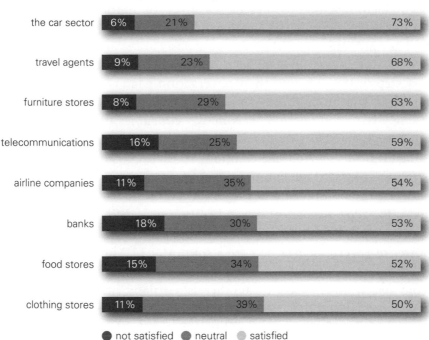

To what extent are you satisfied about...

	not satisfied	neutral	satisfied
the car sector	6%	21%	73%
travel agents	9%	23%	68%
furniture stores	8%	29%	63%
telecommunications	16%	25%	59%
airline companies	11%	35%	54%
banks	18%	30%	53%
food stores	15%	34%	52%
clothing stores	11%	39%	50%

● not satisfied ● neutral ● satisfied

is generally positive. This has also been confirmed by research carried out by KellerFay and InSites Consulting. The chance is therefore great that if a manager starts to follow brand conversations online, he will be pleasantly surprised by the number of positive things he discovers.

In view of this fact that word-of-mouth is generally positive, you should be worried if you find out that this is not the case for your brand. If you are regularly confronted with negative brand feedback, try to establish exactly what people are saying and why – and then put it right!

The Conversation Manager's creed: Brand – Activation – Conversation

The brand is central to the working methods of the Conversation Manager. Everything begins and ends with the brand. Everything stands or falls with the brand. If consumers feel a high degree of identification with your brand, they will be willing to commit to it. Brand identification provides a lever effect for all forms of communication. Both communication emanating directly from the brand, as well as communication which spontaneously arises in consumer circles, will be more powerful if the level of brand commitment is high. The first step in the policy of the Conversation Manager is therefore to establish a clear market position. This positioning should be consistent over a long period. This makes consumer identification that much easier, whereas frequent changes in image make it much more difficult. Brands encourage emotions in their consumers. It is therefore wise to use these emotions to cement the positive relationship between the consumer and the brand. Why do all teenagers want an Apple iPod instead of any other brand of MP3-player? Simply because their brand identification with Apple is greater. Can a supporter of Liverpool ever become a supporter of Manchester United? Almost certainly not. Brand identification is so intense that a change from one football team to another is virtually impossible. Harley Davidson riders often tattoo the Harley badge on their arm – a gesture of brand identification which it is difficult to beat. Millions of consumers prefer Heinz ketchup to any other kind of ketchup, even though many of the others are cheaper. The emotion which the Heinz brand creates results in positive purchasing motivation.

Conversation Managers can influence the position of their brand, amongst other things, through the use of relevant advertising. A Conversation Manager continues to be an advertiser. However, the manner in which he advertises is radically different in comparison with his predecessors. For a Conversation Manager, the purpose of advertising is to activate.

A traditional advertiser regards reach as the most important performance indicator for his campaign. For a Conversation Manager reach is just one of the factors contributing towards his success. Reach – bringing your advert to the attention of your consumers – is the easiest part of advertising. Making sure that the consumer reacts to your message in a positive manner, so much so that he is prepared to pass it on to others, is much more difficult. It is only then that your message will achieve real impact. In other words, the real objective is to activate your consumers, so that they act as secondary advertisers for the promotion of your brand. A high level of activation inevitably leads to an increase in brand indicators (familiarity, preference, etc) and in sales results.[81] In short, we advertise in order to feed the conversation process. The channels chosen by the consumer to carry on this conversation are of less importance.

The Conversation Manager takes account of his consumers' conversations. For this reason, advertising today also means managing these conversations. Most companies nowadays have a PR-manager who carefully monitors press releases. This is a useful function: a company needs to be aware of what is being said about it in the newspapers or on the television. But it is equally important to know what thousands of consumers are saying about your product on the internet and elsewhere. Hence the need for a Conversation Manager.

The philosophy of the Conversation Manager is based on the four dimensions which characterize the behaviour of the modern consumer. While the traditional advertiser scarcely bothers to take account of these trends, the Conversation Manager makes them the central pillars of his policy.

By managing both online and offline conversations, the Conversation Manager takes due account of the fact that consumers are just as likely to talk about brands in their local pub as they are in their social networks on the internet. Because the Conversation Manager knows that a post-modern nomad reacts selectively towards commercial messages, he ensures that his advertisement contains sufficient food for thought – and discussion. He encourages the consumers to use their impact.

By stimulating conversations between consumers, he gives his advertisement added visibility. The emotional nature of the new consumers fits perfectly with the manner in which the Conversation

Manager thinks about brands. Emotion is the glue between the consumer and the brand. By involving consumers in the creation of brand policy (eg by asking for their input into new product ideas) this emotional bond becomes that much tighter. Involvement leads to commitment. Or to put it another way, you arouse emotion in the consumer by letting him participate in what you do. This will lead to an increase in brand identification.

The interaction between brand identification, conversations and advertisements is the playground of the Conversation Manager. He understands how these three elements relate to each other and strengthen each other. The Conversation Manager sees his brand as an oven, his advertisements as the fire and the conversations as the oxygen that will allow his fire to burn.

Make the brand central: people like brands

From the age of two years onwards[82] children are capable of recognizing brands. They even have a preference for particular brands.[83] The round M of McDonald's and the ears of Mickey Mouse are just two of the brand features that they recognize easily. From an early age we grow up with brands and we like choosing between them. In fact, people of all ages like brands. Like them? We love them!

Brands allow us to take irrational buying decisions. If we were satisfied with a simple, efficient means of transport to get us from point A to point B we would all be driving around in Ladas. But as you may have noticed, there are not all that many Ladas on our roads...

A recent study into buying behaviour concluded that people buy 82 per cent more A-brands than ordinary shop brands.[84] Brands for the categories of alcoholic beverages, personal hygiene products, soft drinks and sweets have the highest A-brand appeal. A-brands have a higher quality image in the minds of most consumers – and this plays a significant role. Their emotional commitment to these brands – largely through their perceived quality – is another key factor.

The Conversation Manager puts the brand at the centre of his strategy because he knows that people believe in brands. The success of Harley Davidson, the continuing popularity of Disney, the election of Obama and the hype surrounding the iPhone are all examples of advertising strategies built around a strong central brand. A brand to

Which statement applies to you?

82%

I buy more A-brands than shop brands

18%

I buy more shop brands than A-brands

which consumers can commit is a brand to which managers can commit, and therefore a brand that will ultimately lead to commercial success.

The brands mentioned in the previous paragraph all have in common the fact that they did not shout their message at the consumer. They did not say: 'We are the biggest and the best!' Instead, they ensured that their brand story was consistent and kept that story close to the consumers and their interests. It is almost as if the consumers were allowed to discover for themselves the values the brands actually stand for. In this way, the story appears to be believable, so that the brand and the consumer move ever nearer to each other.

The brand story transcends mere product thinking. Imagine that you have a choice of talking to two manufacturers. One of them tells you an exciting, romantic story, whereas the other simply wants to introduce his products. Which one would you choose? You probably wouldn't need too much time to reach your decision! Learning to make your brand the subject of an interesting story is the first step on your road to becoming a Conversation Manager. This does not mean that the product is irrelevant. On the contrary, it is impossible to build a good brand around a bad product, no matter how fascinating your story might be. Without a decent product, there can be no branding. Continued success requires a quality product which can be related to the everyday needs of the modern consumer through a quality brand with a quality story.

Harry Potter, a brand that can work magic!

In the book *World Wide Rave*[85] there is a classic example of the manner in which a Conversation Manager made maximum use of the lever provided by her brand. Imagine that you are the marketing director of the Universal Studios in Orlando, Florida (one of the most famous attraction parks in the world). It has just been decided that your park should be expanded with a number of spectacular new attractions based on the theme of 'Harry Potter'. Your job is to announce this news to the world in a way which is guaranteed to send your visitor figures rocketing skyward.

A traditional marketeer would pull out all the stops: lavish TV campaigns, posters along all the major motorways and an exclusive PR-agency to pull all the right media strings. With a budget of several million dollars, this approach could hardly fail. However, Cindy Gordon, the vice-president of New Media Marketing, chose to follow the Conversation Manager approach. The Harry Potter brand is heavily laden with emotion. There are millions of fans, spread right across the globe. The length of the queues at the bookstores on the day when the final novel appeared said it all. J.K. Rowling has sold books in more than 200 countries and in 65 different languages: in total no fewer than 325 million copies of the seven different novels.

To spread the message that 'The Wizarding World of Harry Potter' was coming to Orlando, the team at Universal Studios decided to enlist the help of Harry Potter fans. Working together with J.K. Rowling, Universal selected just seven (!) diehard Potter fanatics. These seven people were invited to attend a secret webcast at midnight on 31 May 2007. The webcast was shot on a film set, live from Dumbledore's study. After the fans had been told what was going on, Universal sent an e-mailing to all the regular visitors to their park. The seven fans immediately set to work to place the news on the various Harry Potter fora and blogs. This meant that by the next morning people all over the world were aware of the spectacular development. The story was soon picked up by the traditional press. As a result, within 14 days (according to Universal's own estimates) some 350 million people had been informed of their plans. By offering seven people something exclusive, they had managed to reach a consumer group equal in size to the entire population of North America. In addition, the budget for this operation was relatively limited. Moreover, the fans were delighted with the way the news had been announced. It was perfectly in keeping with the Harry Potter story. Many confessed that their reaction probably would not have been so positive if they had simply read about the plans in the *New York Times*.

Advertise to feed a conversation

Advertisements continue to be an important weapon in the armoury of a Conversation Manager. Activating consumers is the most important objective of this advertising. Traditional advertisers are above all concerned with reach (the number of people they can contact) and selectivity (the percentage of those contacts in their target group). These are also important parameters for the Conversation Manager, but he wants to take matters another step further. His new – and perhaps most important – criterion for success is the number of people who are prepared to spread his message further to others: this is what really counts.

All available media can be used for these purposes: television, newspapers, internet, individual conversations, etc. However, the use of these media must be chosen in relation to their specific strengths.

In the example of Harry Potter, the message was initially given to just seven super-enthusiastic fans via a webcast. This is also a form of advertising. The manner in which Universal Studios communicated this message encouraged these fans to spread the same message to thousands of others around the world. In other words, Universal played to the specific strengths of its chosen method of communication – the Potter fans.

If you launch an advertising campaign of this kind, your basic philosophy will have an impact on both the evolution and the evaluation of the campaign. Strange as it might sound, it is not really relevant to know what message is remembered by the consumers after they have seen the advertisement. But what they tell others about the advert is all the more meaningful – because what they tell others is the message that remains fixed in the minds of the population as a whole.

When companies like TalkTalk and Virgin Media, two major internet providers in the United Kingdom, want to persuade non-internet users to take out a broadband agreement with their company, it is essential that they use this new kind of marketing philosophy. Consumers who in this modern age still have no internet connection are generally slow on the uptake when it comes to new technology. Almost by definition, they are uncertain in this field and this makes their decision-making process uncertain as well. As you might expect, they will search for information, and this search will take in the advertisements put out by TalkTalk and Virgin Media, as well as brochures and other newspaper spots. When these preliminary investigations are completed, they will still be faced with making a choice between the different providers. But how do they know which one to pick? The answer is simple: by seeking further information from their family and friends. Research amongst non-internet users has shown that recommendations of this kind from family and friends are regarded as the most convincing source of information.[86] In other words, family recommendation is the advertising medium *par excellence* for companies like TalkTalk and Virgin Media – and this is where they concentrate. And what works for them might work equally well for you.

Try to remember this when you are communicating your arguments to your customers. They will use these arguments to strengthen their own personal experiences of your brand, when passing them on to others.

The birth of Kai Mook: a unique event, in more ways than one

On Sunday 17 May 2009, at a quarter to nine in the morning, Kai Mook was born – the first baby elephant ever to be successfully bred and delivered on Belgian soil. The zoo in Antwerp quite rightly called it a unique event. The public was enchanted and in the following days there were long queues just to catch a glimpse of the newly born pachyderm. In fact, it is anticipated that Kai Mook will eventually bring in an extra 200,000 visitors.

But it was not only the birth of Kai Mook that was unique: the communication strategy surrounding it was also fairly special. Anja Stas, the zoo's commercial director, working with the Boondoggle agency, applied all the best principles of Conversation Management. For the first time in history, the public could follow the birth of a baby elephant live via a webcam. This was a clever move. Instead of choosing an obvious, traditional advertising message – 'Come and visit our zoo, because we have a baby elephant that you've really got to see' – they chose a more subtle and more emotional message – 'Something wonderful is about to happen. For the first time ever a baby elephant is going to be born in Belgium, and you can be a part of it. If you want to share in the miracle, just tune in live via our webcam.' This latter approach gave people something to talk about – and to watch. More than 500,000 animal-lovers followed the birth live and the zoo's website received 13,000 messages of congratulations from well-wishers all over the world. The public had been well and truly activated.[87]

Some people will react sceptically to this story, and say that it is easy to set up such a campaign with a cuddly baby elephant as your product. It is certainly undeniable that Kai Mook is unique as a product, but it still took courage to approach his birth that way, since there were potentially lots of things that could have gone wrong. But if we concentrate too much on Kai Mook's uniqueness, we are actually missing the point. In the final analysis every company has something unique, which is capable of moving the emotions of the public. You just need to be able to see what it is and dare to advertise it correctly.

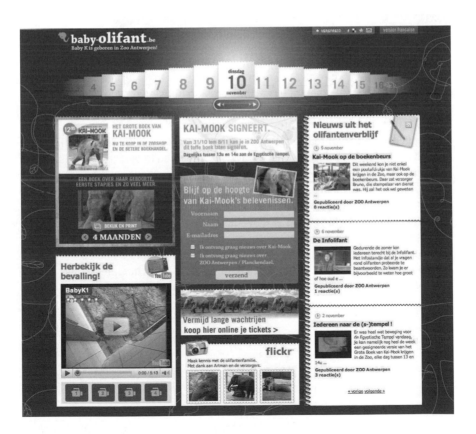

Chiquita awarded Rainforest Alliance Certificate

Chiquita grows bananas with respect for its farmers and respect for the environment. They pay their farmers more than the average rate, they regularly plant replacement trees, they provide housing for the workers in the fields and so on. As a result, the company was recently awarded the Rainforest Alliance Certificate.[88] Chiquita was rightly proud of this recognition, and wanted to share the news with its consumers. Working with the advertising agency These Days, they decided to design a computer game. The game was based on the popular *The Sims* concept. Players were asked to build up and harvest their own plantation, using the same beneficial working methods favoured by Chiquita. The game only lasts five minutes, but some fans have already clocked up more than 200 hours of playing time. In this manner, it is not only possible for the company to advertise its ethical working practices, but the consumers can also experience them at first hand. By allowing people to participate in this way, you give them a message that they can talk about.

Integration of conversations in our daily work

It is very difficult to find marketeers who attach no importance to word-of-mouth. They all understand that consumers can have a

164 million conversations per day and a conversion rate of 30%

Research carried out by InSites Consulting in collaboration with Boondoggle has shown that across the European Union there are some 164 million conversations (of at least 10 minutes' duration) per day about brands.[89] Everyone talks about brands: the young and old, men and women, brand fans and followers as well as those uninterested in brands. The conversations range across almost every product category and thousands of different brands: 66% of these conversations are about the brands themselves, 36% are about branded products and just 11% are about specific communication campaigns. Moreover, the conversations about brands and products carry more impact with other consumers than conversations about advertising. In this respect, 32% of the conversations result in one or more of the participants changing their minds. This confirms that conversations are an important part of the communication mix.

major impact on each other. Yet there are surprisingly few of them who try to integrate word-of-mouth into their marketing strategy. It is a strange, almost inexplicable, contradiction.

It is an elementary feature of the Conversation Manager's way of thinking to always integrate conversations between consumers into everything he does. Consumers are more numerous and more flexible than advertisers. They have no need to take account of politics or hidden agendas. They have no legal department looking over their shoulder, telling them what to do. They say what they mean, and they do what they say – and it is this that determines the success of the brand.

Advertising is intended to give consumers something to talk about. If you understand this, you will already have taken a first step towards managing the resulting conversations. When putting together the design of an advertisement, the initiative for starting the conversation rests with the advertiser. Once the advertisement has appeared, this initiative passes to the consumer. Consumers talk spontaneously about brands. Sometimes they will open discussions about products without there being any real lead-in. The contents of these discussions are valuable for the refinement of products or to offer inspiration for new production ideas.

The managing of conversations consists of listening to interactions between consumers, facilitating their discussions and then daring to intervene in those discussions, so that you speak directly to the people who have opinions about your brand. This last aspect is one of the most difficult tasks of the Conversation Manager: the effective control and direction of conversations with and between consumers.

1,800 films after two weeks

At the beginning of January 2007 Apple organized a press conference. During the presentation, CEO Steve Jobs unveiled the newest Apple innovation: the iPhone. This product launch represented the realization of a personal dream for Jobs. For months in advance there had already been rumours that Apple was about to come on the market with a new cell phone, and now this rumour had become a reality. Steve Jobs showed his prototype to the world, but that was as far as the communication went. The phone itself would only be available for the public in June.

Even so, less than two weeks later a *YouTube* search for the word 'iPhone' called up more than 1,800 different film clips, all made by enthusiastic Apple consumers. By the middle of 2009 the same search called up no fewer than 256,000 clips. The number of online conversations were almost beyond counting. This was an ideal platform to allow Apple to assess initial reaction to its new product. And it soon became clear that there were a number of specific polarities in these conversations: many people were excitedly enthusiastic, whereas others posed a variety of critical questions. The design of the iPhone was described as being stylish and sexy, which in many people's eyes were its strongest points. The issues of greatest concern were the likely battery life and the low resolution of the camera.[90] By studying this information Apple was able to improve its existing product and develop new software updates. This strong market identity promotes involvement. It was almost as if the consumers were lined up waiting for the iPhone launch, just so that they could start giving their feedback to each other and to the company. The process began immediately after the Jobs press conference, and long before the product was on the market. In this sense, the press conference was a form of advertising: the world was told of a new Apple triumph and the consumers were offered a ready-made subject for discussion. It was a perfect example of Conversation Management: give the people something to talk about, monitor their reaction and adjust your product accordingly.

The value of a recommendation

With his book *The ultimate question: driving good profits and true growth*[91] Fred Reichheld has set a new standard in the field of word-of-mouth communication. The ultimate question is: 'to what extent would you be prepared to recommend product X to your friends or colleagues?' Customers can answer on the basis of a score between 0 and 10. The 'detractors' (= people who give scores between 0 and 6) are deducted from the 'active promoters' (= people who give scores of 9 or 10) to calculate the Net Promoter Score (NPS). Reichheld's extensive research proves that there is a correlation between the NPS and the sustainable long-term growth of a company. But how can the value of a recommendation be measured in concrete terms? This is dependent upon the proportion of the sales which are generated by word-of-mouth.

The following example should make things clearer. Computer manufacturer Dell knows that 20 per cent of their customers choose their products because of a recommendation from another Dell customer. On the basis of an average purchase value per customer (US$ 210 in Dell's case) Reichheld estimates the value of each recommendation at US$ 42. If Dell can persuade more people to actively promote its brand, this percentage will increase correspondingly.

In traditional marketing our most valued customers are those who purchase the most. These are also important customers for the Conversation Manager, but not necessarily the most important. According to an article by Kumar, Petersen and Leone the relationship between high frequency of purchase and high recommendation to purchase is not strongly correlated.[92] Their research showed that people who purchase less frequently can sometimes have a higher NPS rating. The financial value of these customers is comparable with the group of customers who buy more frequently but do not actually promote

Conversations in the world of optical laser correction

VisionClinics is the largest clinic for laser-based eye surgery in The Netherlands. On average, they deal with some 4,000 patients each year (which is roughly equivalent to 7,000 to 8,000 individual operations). After the treatment, the patient can say goodbye to the wearing of glasses or contact lenses.

Are conversations and word-of-mouth important in this sector? A customer normally visits the clinic for just one session of treatment, and then his problem is permanently solved. Is there any value in investing in word-of-moth for a customer who is unlikely ever to return? VisionClinics believes that there is. The management teams of private hospitals invest considerable time, effort and money to ensure positive user experience for their customers. In particular, they have a unique understanding of the underlying motives of their patients. The communication with the customer always takes place through the same channel (the hospital). The motives for being in the hospital can vary, according to the patient's individual circumstances. Someone who comes for an exploratory consultation has totally different expectations to someone who comes for a preliminary examination. In the first case, the question of the customer is: 'Can I be helped?' In the second case, the question is: 'What exactly are you going to do?' On the day of the operation this question changes to: 'Has the treatment worked?' VisionClinics takes account of the different needs and different expectations of all its patients and they seek to achieve positive patient experience during every moment of contact. Largely as a result of this approach, 40% of their customers/patients come from personal recommendations. The average cost of treatment is roughly 1,500 euros per eye. If we assume that, with other costs, the patient's bill comes to say 2,250 euros, then the referral value per patient is equivalent to 900 euros (according to the Reichheld method). With 8,000 treatments per year, their total referral value is worth 7.2 million euros.

the brand. In the study, both these groups were exactly the same size: 29 per cent of customers bought regularly but made few recommendations to others and 29 per cent purchased relatively little but made frequent recommendations to others. To describe these groups, the authors coined the new terms 'referral value' and 'monetary value'.

A Conversation Manager cherishes the value of a recommendation and works closely with the customers who view his company positively.

Investing time and energy in people who are favourable to your brand yields a high return. Through their recommendation to others, so called 'less important' customers can bring considerable financial benefit. It is clear that in this manner investment in a positive NPS can influence a company's turnover. A study by the London School of Economics[93] tested the impact of fluctuating NPS on four large companies: HSBC, Asda, Honda and O2. An increase of one NPS point resulted in additional turnover of £8.82 million. A fall of one NPS point resulted in a loss to the company of £ 24.8 million.

NPS: more than a simple KPI

The current popularity of the Net Promoter Score is immense. Almost every company and every brand asks the question 'to what extent would you be prepared to recommend product X to your friends or colleagues' in their market research surveys. The scores resulting from the answers are now quoted as a figure between –100 and +100, this having replaced the average satisfaction rating between 1 and 10. A satisfaction rating or an NPS are important statistics for any organization to have. But they are of little use if you fail to examine the deeper motivating factors which lie behind these scores. Moreover, it is important to remember that every performance indicator has its limitations. Consequently, the NPS system has both supporters and detractors. A study by the scientific magazine *The Journal of Marketing*[94] was unable to confirm the superiority of NPS.

These types of statistics serve as a useful reference point. But it is what you actually do with the statistics that makes the difference. A traditional marketer regards the Net Promoter Score as a trendy new figure to include in his quarterly report, but then does little else. A Conversation Manager seeks to encourage a Net Promoter culture throughout his team. If everybody understands the philosophy behind the NPS, it can be a powerful tool to motivate your sales staff.

A Net Promoter culture places positive consumer experience at the heart of its thinking. Positive experiences lead to positive recommendations, which unquestionably assist the growth of your company.

THE KEY POINTS IN THIS CHAPTER

- The traditional manner of advertising no longer serves to please or placate modern consumers. A new way of working is urgently needed. The philosophy of the Conversation Manager takes account of the four dimensions which characterize today's consumers.

- *'The brand is central'* is the main element in the thinking of the Conversation Manager. The brand can create levers to stimulate conversations. This leads to higher brand performance. As soon as consumers identify with a brand, an interaction develops between brand and consumer. This has a positive effect on sales figures.

- A traditional advertiser seeks to build his brand by forcing his message down his consumers' throats. *The aim of the Conversation Manager is to enter into dialogue, to start a conversation with the consumer.* The consumer is not the end point of the advertisement, but rather the starting point. If an advertisement reaches a consumer but does not prompt him to action, the advertisement has not had maximal impact.

- *Integrating conversations into daily practice* is a key characteristic of the Conversation Manager. Encouraging recommendations, asking for feedback, talking to consumers: these are all important aspects of Conversation Management. Monitoring conversations between consumers and daring to intervene in those conversations is part of his job description.

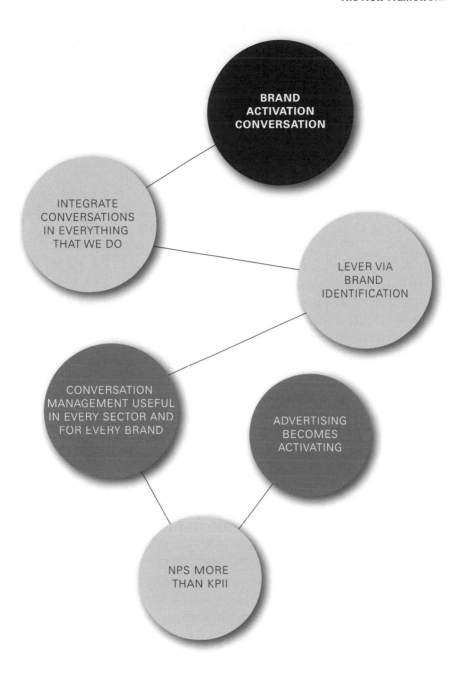

Chapter Four
Your brand deserves a lever

Dealing with the brand paradox

People love brands. People like talking about brands. People are prepared to commit themselves to brands. On the other hand, people are no longer as forgiving towards brands as they used to be. Brand loyalty has been falling, year after year. Fifty-three per cent of consumers have changed one or more of their suppliers during the past six months.[95] This is the brand paradox: on the one hand people are prepared to commit to a brand, while on the other hand consumer loyalty is waning. The challenge of the Conversation Manager is to overcome this paradox: to continue to ensure consumer commitment, while at the same time maintaining consumer loyalty. To deal with this paradox successfully, the Conversation Manager must first understand how consumers interact with brands.

Consumers use social networks as channels of communication to support their own market identity. In this respect, brands colour the personality of the consumer. Some even take this process a stage further, and actually 'lie' about some of their brand acquisitions. In one qualitative research investigation we were told about a person who buys just one bottle of Vittel water. When the bottle is empty, he fills it from the tap to give the impression to his friends that he always drinks branded water. Similarly, in the UK 12 per cent of consumers wear fake brand-label clothing.[96] The most popular fake brands are Burberry and Gucci. Trend-watchers have also noticed the growth of phoney holidays. There are a growing number of people in many lands who say that they go on holiday to exotic destinations, when in fact they simply nip down to the local solarium and get their holiday snaps from *Google* and *Flickr*. This prevents them from losing face in the eyes of their friends.[97]

Consumers see brands as having emotional value. Al Ries and Jack Trout were already saying it before the turn of the century: 'Marketing is not a battle between products, it is a battle of perceptions.'[98] As long ago as 1994 they were advising market managers not to be so 'rational' in their approach to their brands. 'Marketing managers control facts and analyse situations in order to make the truth suit their own purposes. They then step into the marketing arena, full of confidence. They are certain that they have the best product, are convinced that they are going to win the battle for customers. But it is an illusion, there is no objective reality. There are only perceptions. Perception is reality, and all the rest is illusion,' say Ries and Trout. The emotional value also ensures that consumers are prepared to build up a relationship with a brand. Scientific research by Fournier has shown that consumers regard brands as valuable 'life-partners'. And the relationship between the consumer and the brand becomes even stronger if the consumer can experience various different aspects of the brand.[99] In particular, brand experience becomes more intense in relation to the degree that the consumer is able to detect and absorb the brand with his different senses.[100] Singapore Airlines is the air operator which pays most attention to the sensory perception of its passengers. Each plane is perfumed with exactly the same fragrance and each plane plays exactly the same recorded music. The hostesses are dressed and made up in exactly the same manner, so that they create a recognizable image. All the senses of the passengers are stimulated in a consistent manner, so that an emotional bond is formed. It is no coincidence that Singapore Airlines is the aviation company with the most satisfied customers.[101]

The Conversation Manager takes full account of the behaviour of the smart and emotional consumer. For this reason, product management is less important than the creation of brand experience. Of course, good products will always be necessary to make your company successful, but they are really a minimum condition. It is brand experience which determines whether or not the consumer wants to take part in the story you have created for him.

You can't replace Mickey Mouse just like that

The Donaldson clothing brand was founded in 1983. Donaldson clothes were famous for their use of a Mickey Mouse logo, and the two were often mentioned in the same breath. Every jersey, coat, skirt or pair of trousers was embroidered with Disney's most famous cartoon figure. The brand had success in several European markets, but at the end of 2007 Donaldson decided to put an end to their collaboration with Disney. According to managing director Cocquelet, there were three reasons for this surprising decision.[102]

Firstly, Mickey was no longer the symbol of the American dream (at least according to Cocquelet). Since the opening of the Disney park near Paris, visiting Disneyland is no longer out of reach for the average European family. Secondly, the collaboration with Disney was no longer exclusive: C&A also had a deal for an assortment of Disney products with Mickey Mouse. Thirdly, the termination of the Disney contract was financially beneficial (although this, it was claimed, was not the most important reason).

And so it was that Mickey Mouse was shown the door. From January 2008 onwards he was replaced by a new Donaldson logo: a cute little doggie. But not cute enough. Ten months later Donaldson filed for bankruptcy.[103] There were clearly other reasons for the company's rapid demise, but the new logo was the straw which finally broke the camel's back. All consumer association with the brand was lost almost overnight. For many people, the Mickey Mouse figure was a key element in their willingness to commit to Donaldson – as soon became clear from a survey conducted amongst ex-Donaldson fans. Changing the logo broke the crucial emotional relationship between consumer and brand. Brand identity is a precious commodity, and should not be played with lightly. Changing a fundamental element of your brand should only be undertaken after close consultation with your consumers. And the replacement for this element must be able to inspire the same levels of consumer involvement and commitment.

Branding is emotion!
Kinder Surprise makes us smile!

The emotional experience of a brand determines the intensity of the relationship between the brand and the consumer.[104] However, our current method of advertising is more closely based on the rational aspects of the brand. The Interbrand top 100 is a good example of this. Each year Interbrand uses a complex formula to calculate the financial worth of the most valuable brands in the world. Coca-Cola is the most valuable of all in this ranking, with an estimated Interbrand value of no less than US$ 66.7bn. The other companies in the top five are IBM, Microsoft, General Electric and Nokia.[105] No doubt this rational valuation is useful for managers and business economists. However...

In view of the fact that the Conversation Manager above all wishes to know the current strength of the emotional relationship between the consumer and his brand, we also need to develop an emotional value indicator. At the moment, there is no standard formula for the assessment of such emotional factors, but the following are examples of possible indicators which can be used:

- The first possibility is the *sensory excellence test* developed by Martin Lindstrom.[106] This test checks the extent to which brands make use of all the senses in order to provide the consumer with a consistent, all-embracing brand experience. Lindstrom applied his test criteria to the top-200 Interbrand companies. Only 10 per cent of these companies are actively concerned with this kind of all-round sensory approach. The toppers in this respect are: Singapore Airlines, Apple, Disney, Mercedes-Benz and Marlboro.

- The second possibility is to monitor how frequently your brand is mentioned in blogs. A brand which is being written about is a brand which interests people and arouses their curiosity. In February 2010 we conducted a small test on the website blogpulse.com. Who do you think was the most talked about person between December 2009 and February 2010: Roger Federer (who had just won his sixteenth Grand-slam event at Wimbledon), Michael Phelps (the Olympic legend) or Christiano Ronaldo (the most expensive footballer in the world)? Who had the highest blog intensity? The answer is Roger Federer. The average blog activity for Federer was comparable with Michael Phelps. Phelps come second, because the intensity of the activity was much higher for Federer: tennis as a sport still excites people more than swimming, even at Olympic level. Christiano Ronaldo was only mentioned in comparison with the other two.

- The third possibility is also the simplest. Just see how many fans the brand has on *Facebook*, because *Facebook* is also an indicator

of emotional brand experience. Using this method of assessment, the top-five most popular brands vary dramatically with the Interbrand list. Only Coca-Cola is included in both rankings.[107] The *Facebook* top-five reads as follows: Starbucks (6 million fans), Coca-Cola (5 million), Nutella (3.2 million), *YouTube* (3 million) and, last but not least, Kinder Surprise (2.6 million). By comparison, Nokia (the fourth most valuable 'rational' brand in the world) has just 600,000 fans on *Facebook*.

Kinder Surprise is a remarkable brand. If I show a photograph of a Kinder Surprise egg during one of my presentations, it is noticeable how all the faces in the room begin to smile. It somehow seems to conjure up happy memories and emotions in all of us. Last year I came across just two participants who had never eaten a Kinder Surprise. What does all this popularity signify? Who can say, but it is obviously an indication of emotional commitment. Moreover, the fans on *Facebook* make it perfectly clear that they are precisely that: fans – they say so in as many words and they say it to all their friends. Or to put it another way, the brand helps the consumer to define and strengthen his own personal brand identity.

Apple makes you creative

Researchers at Duke University and Canada's University of Waterloo have proven that people are more capable of creative thought when they see the Apple logo than when they see the IBM logo.[108] This effect is evident after consumers have seen the logo for just thirty milliseconds.

The research team asked the test persons to develop creative applications for a common-or-garden brick. The guinea pigs were divided into two groups: one group was shown the Apple logo, and the other the IBM logo. The IBM group were only able to devise applications where more than one brick was needed. The results of the Apple group were both more numerous and more creative: eight useable ideas against the five suggestions made by the IBM group. In total 341 students took part in these experiments and the trend in the results was confirmed time after time. Much the same results were achieved if the Apple logo was replaced by a Disney logo.

The Conversation Manager can employ one or more of these emotional value indicators, using the resulting figures to interpret trends and plan actions.

Brand identification creates a lever effect

Traditional models to measure the strength of a brand usually place the emphasis on value and image. The assessment takes account of knowledge,[109] familiarity, brand loyalty[110] and brand perception.[111] More recently, the level of positive recommendations was also added to this list.[112] Before this, none of the available branding models took the conversations of consumers about brands into consideration. Based on practical experience and the results of various customer projects, the hypothesis was put forward that intense brand identification should stimulate the number of positive conversations about that brand. This result should also lead to the better performance of the brand.

Based on this hypothesis, InSites Consulting carried out a study, in collaboration with Houston University in the USA. In total 5,921 persons took part in the study, originating from 15 countries spread across Europe (Belgium, Denmark, France, Italy, The

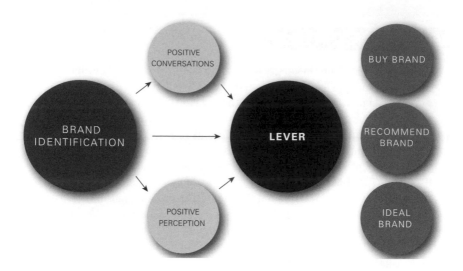

Netherlands, Poland, Romania, Slovakia, Spain, Turkey, Sweden and Switzerland) and the United States.[113] The purpose of the investigation was to see if our ideas about brand experience and modern consumers were correct. The brand experiences provided by 10 worldwide brands were used as a test case.

The results of the study were identical for all countries and for all brands. The study therefore confirmed the hypothesis beyond a shadow of a doubt: a high level of brand identification results in a greater number of positive conversations about that brand. Equally important, a high level of brand identification results in a better perception of the brand.

The impact of these three elements is considerable: brand identification, positive brand conversations and better brand perception all have a lever effect on brand performance. If a brand has a good score for these three marketing dimensions, consumers will buy the brand more frequently and recommend it to others more often. It is almost as if it becomes an 'ideal' brand. The key to all these levers is the brand identification: if people can see their own personal values (or aspirational values) in the brand, this will be enough to initiate the lever effect. A further conclusion from the study revealed that the importance of consumer conversations is much higher in countries with higher levels of internet penetration. The more active consumers are on the net, the more important word-of-mouth becomes.

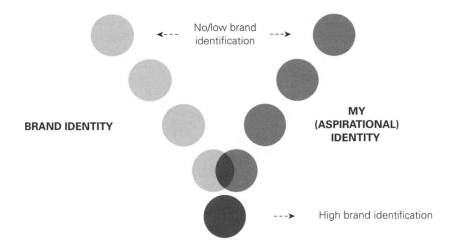

Brand identification is the heart and soul of Conversation Management. The results of this study teach us that positive word-of-mouth is difficult to achieve if consumers are not able to identify with your brand. Brands such as Starbucks, Lego, Nike, Obama, Kinder Surprise and Harry Potter all have a strong relationship with their consumers. They are all brands that have earned their status. Brand identification is the key to the lever effect, but it is not something that happens overnight. For this reason, persistence and vision are two of the most crucial qualities for a Conversation Manager. 'In addition to great marketing dedication and a heap of money, I also needed twenty years to build a brand,' said Karel Vuursteen, former director of Heineken.[114]

Brand identification is very fragile. People do not easily identify themselves with a brand, which means that the relationship can easily be damaged. At the end of 2009 it became clear that Tiger Woods was not the ideal son-in-law he had once seemed, and his addiction to sex has cost him dearly. Numerous companies had hitched their wagon to his star in recent years: Tiger was believed to have almost the perfect sporting image, an image that millions wanted to identify with. This was not lost on the brands which queued up to make sponsoring and advertising deals with the world's best golfer. Some of these brands were also in the world class: Nike, Gatorade and Gillette, for example.

When the sex scandal broke, these companies hesitated to maintain their link with Woods. There was a real possibility that many people's identification with the brand through the sportsman would have been negatively affected by his recent escapades. With this possibility in mind, the YouGov research bureau[115] investigated the impact of the Tiger Woods media storm on the public perception of these brands.

In particular, Nike's image was severely dented. The general perception of the brand, especially with women, took a nosedive. The brand perception stabilized several weeks later, but at a level much lower than before the controversy began. Gillette also experienced negative brand impact. As with Nike, brand perception suffered badly. Worried by this development, Gillette immediately reduced its collaboration with Woods. The effect was immediate, and their image was restored in a matter of weeks to its former level. Gatorade was even more drastic: they terminated their sponsoring contract with the golfer. In reality, this decision had already been taken before the media storm broke, but it certainly influenced the timing of the announcement. By distancing themselves from the fallen idol in this manner, the perception of their brand in the market was given a considerable boost.

Brand identification is of fundamental importance for a Conversation Manager. It is the foundation upon which all his activities are built. If it is threatened, he must act promptly and decisively to protect and preserve it.

What can a brand learn from a football team?

I am a supporter of FC Bruges. Since my fifteenth birthday I have been a season-ticket holder at my favourite club. The period 2006–09 was not a particularly happy one for Bruges fans. The commercial analysis of this period shows that the club offended against all the laws of traditional marketing. The quality of the product – like the team's position in the league – dropped significantly. The number of games won with a difference of two goals or more could be counted on the fingers of one hand. More games against the other top teams were lost rather than won. Customer service also suffered. Lucrative television deals meant that the kick-off times changed frequently, so that the 23,000 loyal fans had difficulty keeping track of the day, let alone the time, when the game was scheduled. Yet in spite of all these negative factors, the price of a season ticket kept rising, year after

> ## Le Pain Quotidien grows through brand identification
>
> Le Pain Quotidien is a brand that stands for fun but biologically-responsible eating. It is also a brand that in recent years has shown a very 'healthy' growth curve. Le Pain Quotidien currently has 130 shops spread across the globe, from Sydney to New York.
>
> This growth can be explained by a strong focus on a particular culture and philosophy. The shops all exude the same warm and friendly atmosphere. There are newspapers to read, there are crumbs on the tables, there are pots of jam lying everywhere. It's just like home! The food is tasty and biological. As a result, many of their customers are from the higher social classes, who are generally more concerned with healthy eating and who are more likely to want to read the papers while sipping their heartwarming cup of coffee. These people identify fully with the values of Le Pain Quotidien – and pass the news on to their friends.

year. Product quality down, customer service down and prices up? That's not the way things are supposed to work! Imagine what would happen if you tried that strategy with your own brand! The effect would be disastrous. But for FC Bruges the opposite seems to be true. For the 2009–10 season their number of loyal customers, expressed in season-ticket sales, has risen again.[116] Moreover, in 2009 FC Bruges was again chosen as the most popular sports brand in Belgium. It was the fourth most popular of all brands.[117]

How is it possible to explain this phenomenon? One hypothesis (largely circulated by fans of rival team Anderlecht) is that the supporters of FC Bruges are all barmy. Another, more plausible hypothesis is that there are other factors which are more important than product and service quality, which continue to attract people to the Jan Breydel Stadium. And by far and away the most important of these other factors is brand identification. Football is the only commercial category where consumers talk of 'we' instead of 'me'. If you go to a pop concert, you never say: 'We sung well.' Your reaction after a concert is confined to an evaluation of the artist's performance, even though you and many others will have been singing along for most of the time. At a football match, crowd participation is focused on eating hamburgers and drinking beer. True, this does

The Harley Davidson KPI: the number of tattoos

There are many different ways to build up a strong and distinctive image through branding. Football fans often wear a scarf in their favourite team's colours. BMW fans frequently have a key ring displaying their favourite car make. The tattooing of your body is perhaps a more extreme way to demonstrate your brand loyalty. A tattoo is for life, so before you have it done you need to be certain that the values of the brand are in perfect agreement with your own personal lifestyle and philosophy. Harley Davidson is a brand which many people feel able to identify with. The annual report of the motorbike manufacturer proudly boasts: 'Retention is for wimps. We measure the percent of customers who have our name tattooed on one of their body parts.'[118]

encourage participative singing (of a kind!) on the terraces, but no one actually gets out on the field and starts playing football. And yet afterwards everybody talks about the game in the 'we' form. 'We played well.' 'We're going to win the league.' 'We ought to shoot the manager.' These are all typical comments that you can hear from the supporters in the course of an average season.

Evarist Moonen, the commercial director at FC Bruges, has noticed a trend which might help to explain all these seemingly 'irrational' but commercially significant developments. 'The arrival of online communities allows people to commit more easily to the club. And this commitment in turn allows them to make the transition from "spectator" to "supporter".' If people can feel involved in a brand story, their dedication towards that brand will increase.

So what can a Conversation Manager learn from a football team? That brand identification transcends product quality. And that consequently it is important to involve people in the policy relating to that brand. Because football fans are able to contribute to the policy of their favourite club, either directly (via supporters groups) or indirectly (by singing on the terraces), their commitment to their team increases. Online communities are an ideal platform for involving and mobilizing large numbers of people behind their favourite 'brand'.

Toyota: the broken lever

For many years Toyota lived in motoring paradise: there was a high satisfaction level amongst its brand's many drivers. Research by the KellerFay Group showed that Toyota was the brand with the most positive word-of-mouth on a worldwide scale.[119] However, at the beginning of 2010 Fate came knocking at the door. And the problems that Fate brought with her were real beauties. There was a problem with the gas pedal, which could cause cars to accelerate unexpectedly. There was also a serious brake defect with the Prius model (the flagship of the Toyota range, a hybrid car which fits perfectly with today's increasingly important environmental trends).

In addition to the technical problems, their brand communication was also sub-standard. Local Toyota offices received little or no information from their headquarters in Japan. This meant that information was also slow to reach the customers. Finally, the top man of Toyota called a press conference to clarify some of these important matters, but as soon as the journalists started to ask critical questions he sped away in his car – an Audi!

Everyone knows that in time of crisis there is only one good communication strategy that really works: the truth, the whole truth and nothing but the truth. Complete transparency is the only option. Unfortunately, Toyota chose a different path. On their corporate website they continued to promote models that were not recalled. Selling cars – at all costs, it seems – continued to be their highest priority. This was a bad move: it was almost like laughing in the face of the customers. The people surfing the site were not stupid: they were all too well aware that the company was facing fundamental problems. Yet Toyota behaved as though the problems didn't exist, whereas they would have been much better advised to devote their whole website to these key issues.

The identification between the brand and its consumers was badly dented. Positive word-of-mouth was replaced by thousands of negative reactions. Toyota can only restore damaged confidence by delivering a new range of top-quality products and by building up a more consistent manner of communication with its consumers.

It is regrettable that in this difficult situation Toyota neglected to make use of the power of its many fans. When the crisis began, Toyota had about 75,000 fans on *Facebook*. If things start to go wrong, these enthusiastic people can play an important role in your communication strategy. Yet Toyota chose not to enlist the help of these loyal supporters of its brand. Instead, they preferred to rely on more traditional forms of communication, such as newspapers. Of course, it is important to use these traditional channels as well, but it is much better to speak to your own fans directly. This way, you hear the first reactions of people who are positively inclined towards you. More importantly, you hear their questions and concerns. This allows you to keep your eye on the ball, so that you can act quickly – and deal with the right things. One general conclusion that we can draw from the Toyota debacle (although it is applicable to all brands) is that you should prepare your crisis communication strategy before the crisis actually arrives. Working proactively with a large fan community is becoming increasingly necessary. Fans are your most important communication channel in moments of real crisis. If you explain to them what is going on and if you involve them in the search for a solution, you will find yourself in a much stronger position.

Domino's Pizza: listening as the basis for a new lever[120]

Domino's Pizza was confronted with negative buzz in various social media. Customers twittered loud and long that the crusts on their pizza tasted like cardboard. In official pizza rankings Domino's stood consistently near (or at) the bottom of the table. Domino's listened to this negative word-of-mouth and decided to try and do something about it. The first step in their battle to rebuild their brand was to listen to the consumers. They examined the feedback that was available online and organized a number of focus groups with customers. In this way they were able to gather detailed and accurate information about the current problems with their brand.

The results made sorry reading for Domino's. The quality of the pizza was regarded as little short of disastrous. Even so, the management bounced back strongly. First, they accepted that there was a problem: the perception of the customer is the only reality. Next, they analysed the feedback. As a result, a number of teams were put together to work on all aspects of the pizza's quality: the crust needed to be improved, the basic sauce needed to be spicier, the toppings needed stronger flavours and even the cheese had to be tangier.

The results were not long in coming: everything was improved so that the pizzas (probably for the first time) now actually tasted like pizza – at least according to the product development team. But how would the focus groups react: this would be the real test. Happily, the focus groups agreed – and asked for more.

The communication strategy for rebuilding the brand was also very open. The company made a video film which included extracts from the negative *Twitter* messages and the critical comments of the focus groups. It then showed step-by-step how efforts had been made to deal with each of these criticisms. The film was distributed via various social media, such as *YouTube* and *Twitter*, and in less than a month's time no fewer than 500,000 people had seen the new Domino message (which lasted four minutes!).

This campaign, in spite of its success, is simply the beginning of a long road for Domino's. The company was once one of the fastest growing fast-food chains in the world, but its market leverage has been severely damaged over the years because of the falling quality of its products. By listening to its consumers and communicating with them in a transparent manner, it has been possible to create a new lever. But there is still a lot of work to be done: you can't rebuild a brand overnight.

Brand identification is the priority of the Conversation Manager

The Conversation Manager understands that positive conversations are not possible without identification between the brand and the consumer. Mapping out and analysing the identification gap which may still exist between the brand and the consumer is therefore their highest priority.

The only way to develop successful brand identification is through a long-term vision. Moreover, this vision needs to be consistently applied. Disney is a good example of a brand with which the public can easily and clearly identify. For more than 70 years Disney has been consistent in every aspect of its communication. Its animation films are still warm and positive stories with a happy ending. Disney avoids all forms of controversy. It has no axe to grind: it is in the business of entertaining people and making them feel good. Its parks reflect this aim and perfectly mirror the atmosphere of the films. Every Disney theme park, no matter where it is, is instantly familiar in terms of ambiance and style. Years of consistent policy have resulted in high visibility and instant recognition – and these are the key factors which lead to brand identification.

Some years ago, the *Harvard Business Review*[121] posed a highly pertinent question: 'If the building of brands requires years of effort, why are companies managed on a quarterly basis?' There is a great temptation to try and improve the short-term results of a brand through smart sales promotions. But measuring the results of a long-term strategy is much more difficult. In my opinion, many brands are not really managed, but are made the subject of specific careers and their development. In a large company the product manager will be in charge of a brand for perhaps two to three years at most. But the creation and implementation of a vision takes much longer than that. The danger is that the strategy will be changed every time that the post-holder changes.

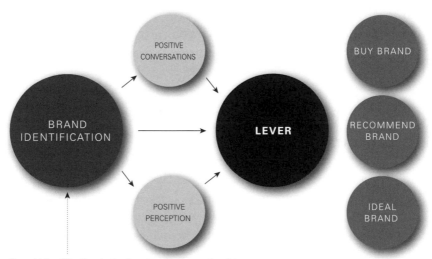

Brand identification is the heart of Conversation Management.

The Conversation Manager commits himself to his brand over a longer period. He can keep an eye on the short-term results, whilst at the same time seeking to achieve long-term growth. Understanding the workings of brand identification is his first key step along this road. The second is the decision about the values for which his brand will stand. The third and final step is the hardest: years of continuous effort to get his brand to the desired position – and then to keep it there.

THE KEY POINTS IN THIS CHAPTER

- The Conversation Manager must learn to deal with the brand paradox. People love brands, but at the same time can be quite scathing towards them. They have no problem in committing to a brand, but if things go wrong they will be quick to switch to another. *Consumers are loyal – but not unconditionally.*

- *Consumers look at brands emotionally.* Both online and offline, people want to bond with the brands that they really like. Moreover, they use their favourite brands to give better definition to their own personal market positioning. Advertisers manage their brands too rationally and often forget the great emotional power which is inherent in all good brands.

- *The Conversation Manager tries to keep the gap between market identity and the (aspirational) identity of the consumer as small as possible.* If a consumer identifies with a brand, then the number of positive conversations relating to that brand will increase and the brand perception will improve. More positive conversations, better market perceptions and a strong brand identity all help to create a lever for the brand. This lever results in higher sales figures and a higher Net Promoter Score. As a result, the consumer will increasingly see the product as being 'ideal'.

- Advertisers can learn a lot from football. Football teams enjoy the highest levels of brand identification. *Extreme brand identification ensures that consumers will no longer switch between brands.*

CONSUMERS USE
BRANDS TO
POSITION
THEMSELVES

BRAND
IDENTIFICATION
IS THE HEART OF
CONVERSATION
MANAGEMENT

IDENTIFICATION
CREATES
COMMITMENT
TO BRANDS

NO CONVERSATION
WITHOUT
IDENTIFICATION

Chapter Five
Advertising becomes activating

Activation is central

In *The Tipping Point*,[122] a best-seller about social epidemics, Malcolm Gladwell tells the story of silversmith Paul Revere. On a sunny spring day in 1775, Revere heard rumours that the British army was planning to launch a surprise attack against local resistance leaders and their units. He rode from village to village, spreading the news. During this famous 'midnight ride' he managed to mobilize all those opposed to British rule. As a result, the Americans were able to beat the British in battle next day. And so the American Revolution was started. Gladwell attributes Paul Revere's success to the fact that he was a convincing sales person (a useful talent for a silversmith). Equally important, he knew many of the people he was talking to and he was obviously sincere in what he was saying. Word-of-mouth is as old as mankind.

Gladwell's theory puts forward personal characteristics as the most critical success factors for a word-of-mouth message. According to this theory, only a limited number of unique individuals (who combine a good sales technique with a large network and maximum credibility) have the talent to create impact with word-of-mouth. And indeed much WOM literature focuses on influential figures. However, there are also several theories which cast doubt on the importance of personal charisma. Might not the message of someone you meet on a train or in a pub be just as important?

Different research surveys, including a study carried out by InSites Consulting, prove that the key fact is not 'who does it' but rather 'what they do'.[123] The word-of-mouth market research agency KellerFay[124] came to the same conclusion: as far as WOM is concerned 'what you do' must always be the starting point and not 'who you are'. Both studies show that socio-demographic factors have a limited effect on the degree of activation achieved. Although one person may have more impact than another, it is the actions of the total population which are crucial for the level of activation. This means that in order to devise good campaigns, advertisers need to make the action itself the central element of their strategy, rather than concentrating on the most influential customers. In many ways this is common sense, because it can sometimes be hard in practice to know precisely who is 'the most influential'. Next time you are in a cinema or concert hall, look around you. Who is the most influential person there? It's not easy, is it? Now imagine the problem facing Coca-Cola if they want to try and find the most influential Coke drinker. It's like looking for the proverbial needle in a haystack. But by making the action central, you can apply a concrete and effective activation philosophy.

For a Conversation Manager activation is the main objective of any communication campaign aimed at his target group. Stimulating people to engage in word-of-mouth is a basic principle of every form of advertising. It is only when several thousand children start talking about Harry Potter that the spark will ignite with a new and wider group of readers. These will then share their enthusiasm with yet further groups of adults and children, and before you know it you have sold a couple of million books, like J.K. Rowling. Recently, I asked several of my friends whether or not their children liked watching television programmes from 'our' time. 'Oh yes,' was the most common answer, 'but they find them less fun, because they can't talk to their friends at school about them.' A television programme is only really successful when everyone is talking about it in a positive way.

Activation has a number of different participation levels.[125] The basic level is simply bringing your message to the attention of your target audience – and leaving it at that. This is the traditional indicator of success: how many people have you reached? However, from the moment when your consumer starts spreading your message, you have gone a significant step further. The ultimate form of activation is when the consumer develops his own content in support of your message, and spreads that as well.

These three levels of activation form the core of the InSites Consulting activation model.[126]

- The *receipt of the message* is the lowest step in the activation pyramid. As soon as someone has been exposed to your message and absorbed it, this lowest step has already been climbed. Nowadays, people can receive messages in many different ways, not only via the traditional media but also via films on *YouTube* or participation in online discussion groups. This is the level at which the traditional advertiser evaluates his campaign, but a Conversation Manager needs to look further.

- The second step of the pyramid is *the spreading of the message*. This encompasses the many different ways in which consumers share information with each other about brands and products. A conversation with your friends about your favourite type of beer, describing your night out at a restaurant to your family, recommending a good book to a colleague at work, proudly showing your new cell phone to your fellow students, forwarding an interesting promotional e-mail to the people in your address book: these are all popular examples of activation. The possibilities are endless, and everyone in society is a potential activator.

- The highest step of the activation pyramid is *the creation of new information which supports the brand message*. For instance, consumers can give feedback about their favourite brand via their blog, or perhaps even make a short film about it for *YouTube*. Sounds far-fetched? Eight per cent of the population has already made a film about a brand that has been posted on the video website of *YouTube*. Thirty per cent to 40 per cent have contributed information about brands to the various kinds of online platform (blogs, fora, status updates, etc).[127] In other words, this creative phase is not a step which only relatively few consumers manage to take. Recent research has shown that 55 per cent of consumers would be prepared to develop their own content for a brand.[128]

Our hypothesis about the activation pyramid runs as follows: the broader the top of the pyramid, the better the results of the brand in question will be. And our survey to measure word-of-mouth has confirmed the truth of this hypothesis.[129] Higher activation leads

The Da Vinci Code web-quest[130]

More than 40 million copies of the book *The Da Vinci Code* by Dan Brown have already been sold. In 2006 the long-awaited film of the book was finally launched. Tom Hanks played the leading role of Professor Robert Langdon. To promote the film, it was decided to activate the book's fans by organizing a web-quest. This quest was a joint venture between Google and Sony Pictures. For 24 days, the participants were sent successive pieces of the puzzle which needed to be solved. The first 10,000 people who provided the right answers were allowed to take part in the second stage of the quest. This involved the decoding of a cryptex which contained a URL leading to the final puzzles. The first person to correctly solve these final puzzles was the winner of the quest. The total prize money for the winner was a cool 125,000 dollars. During the competition, the Sony website received 10 times its normal number of visitors.

The campaign was primarily aimed at the real fans of the book, but people who were fascinated by the challenge of solving Professor Langdon-like puzzles also soon joined in – in large numbers. And because of their fascination, this gave them something to talk about with other people, who in turn wanted to see what all the fuss was about. In this way not only were the fans activated, but they in turn activated tens of thousands of others. As a result, the launching of the film was a great success. The pre-sale of cinema tickets began weeks before the actual opening, just as the online quest was reaching its climax. The results exceeded all expectations – even though the film was panned by the critics.

to increased awareness, greater interest and better sales for a brand. The highest levels of impact are achieved by offline word-of-mouth and information from online discussion fora or e-mails. The impact of online videos is more limited.

The danger of activation for activation's sake

Activation is the goal of the Conversation Manager. But there is always a great danger lurking just around the corner with this strategy: activation for activation's sake. By stimulating commitment in your consumers, you strengthen the power of your brand. But campaigns spread by consumers which fail to support the values of brand are useless. Worse, they are counter-productive. A few years ago, the actress Pamela Anderson was used in an advertisement for a Chinese animal rights organization. A photo of Pamela was printed on 70,000 telephone cards. Pamela was topless, but stood with her back to the camera. The message was: 'Cold shoulders are nothing compared to the pain you are causing defenceless animals.' The phone card was hot news and much talked about, but most of the talking was about Pamela – and not about animal rights, which had been the object of the exercise. Activation for activation's sake does not contribute to a stronger brand. The telephone cards were withdrawn from the market because of their 'excessive erotic content'.[131]

Another example: in 2000 Virgin launched a simple pre-paid telephone card on the American market.[132] To promote this launch, the CEO of Virgin performed some 'death-defying' stunts on the Empire State Building, in the hope of attracting attention for his company's new product. He got plenty of attention, alright – but not the kind he was hoping for. Most of the newspapers covered the story, but their main focus of interest was whether Richard Branson was really naked or was he just wearing a flesh-coloured jump suit! The phone card hardly got a mention.

Advertising agencies are sometimes given the task of devising a 'viral campaign' – and those are all the instructions they get! This kind of limited briefing is well meant ('give the creative people their freedom') but the risk of things going pear-shaped is correspondingly large. A briefing must always begin with a definition of the target group and the objective of the campaign. Only then will the advertising agency be able to satisfactorily meet the expectations of the customer. The creative team will try to come up with a well-targeted concept rather than just shooting blindly in the dark. Activation must have a clear purpose – otherwise it loses its effect. Communication objectives – even in this modern day and age – must fit with the brand identity that the company is attempting to portray.[133]

The Conversation Manager puts activation at the heart of his strategy and attaches great importance to brand identification. Activation must contribute towards an even better relationship with the consumer, so as to create a lever effect. Activation without a specific purpose is simply a wasted investment.

> ## Whopper Virgin's campaign causes storm of protest[134]
>
> Burger King, the world's second largest hamburger chain, wanted to persuade consumers through a comparative advertising campaign that their Whopper (the flagship of their burger range) tasted better than the Big Mac (the flagship burger of McDonald's). To make the comparison 'objective' Burger King wanted to organize a tasting with people who had never tried a hamburger before – the so called 'Whopper Virgins'. This was no easy task, certainly in America, and so they travelled (amongst other places) to a remote village in Romania, in order to find a group of people who had so far been deprived of one of civilization's greatest benefits – a juicy American quarter-pounder. The bemused villagers were more than happy to oblige. And can you guess which of the two burgers was unanimously chosen as the tastiest? Of course! The Whopper!
>
> The aim of the campaign was to stimulate people (primarily Americans) to discuss the relative merits of the rival burgers in terms of taste. But the activation rebounded on its creators. The campaign was greeted with a storm of criticism. Most people thought that Burger King (to use an appropriate phrase) had behaved in very bad taste. Some of the tests were actually carried out in regions where the majority of the people were starving. Many Americans were ashamed of a campaign which seemed to emphasize all the very worst stereotypes of their country. The result was a great deal of discussion about the campaign itself, but very little discussion about the original objective: to decide who actually had the best burger.

The three dimensions of good activation

Activation is successful if all the necessary subsidiary conditions are fulfilled. In this respect, the following three dimensions are important:

1 *The profile*: who spreads the message?
2 *The motivation*: why do they spread the message?
3 *The content of the conversation*: what do they say when they are spreading the message?

Before discussing each of these dimensions in detail, it is worth considering the following matters.

The professional literature relating to activation is mainly focused on the profile of the sender. If someone has influence within his

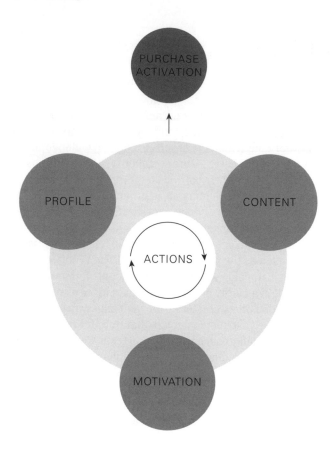

own particular domain, this tends to benefit the impact of the word-of-mouth.[135] This describes the first dimension. In addition, various scientific and academic studies also devote considerable attention to the second dimension, the motives of the sender. The underlying reasons for the activation help to determine the impact of the message.[136] Research by InSites Consulting has confirmed factors which influence the mechanisms of these first two dimensions but has also analysed in detail the nature of the third dimension: the content of the conversations themselves, the message which is passed on to family and friends. This factor is just as important for the impact of the message.[137] All three elements – the profile, the motivation and the contextual message of the sender – can affect the consumer in different ways.

The right people, the right reasons and the right words are the keys to good activation. And for a good Conversation Manager each of these dimensions is equally important.

Dimension 1. Fans and experts build your brand

The first dimension which determines the level of impact of your activation is the profile of the sender. Let us think back to Paul Revere. He succeeded in mobilizing America's resistance to the British. One of his success factors was his credible profile. If you were looking for a good restaurant, how would you go about finding it? Most people would ask someone from their circle of acquaintances who is well-known for his (or her) knowledge of restaurants. Usually, such 'experts' are happy to display their 'wisdom' and would be pleased to recommend you a selection of good restaurants in your neighbourhood. Traditional advertisers only see value in the number of people they are able to reach. In contrast, the Conversation Manager realizes that some consumers can offer their brand more value than others. This added value is normally to be found in the level of influence they possess (see above). Seth Godin regards 'influence' as a more important parameter than reach.[138] People who are quick to try new products are typically more likely to exert a greater influence on those around them. The classic literature relating to the adoption of new products refers to five steps, each linked to a particular group of consumers: innovators, early adopters, early majority, late majority and laggards. Perhaps surprisingly, it is not the *innovators* who activate, but rather the *early adopters*.[139] In particular, the success of high-technology products is heavily dependent upon the extent to which *early adopters* are willing to promote the product to others.[140]

This word-of-mouth reduces the risk perception of the following group in the chain, since the value of the innovative products has already been 'proven' by a previous group of consumers. In this sense, activating consumers are regarded as experts within their specific domain by their fellow consumers. However, the title of 'expert' is only applicable within a very limited area of expertise. Just because you know everything about local restaurants does not mean that you know anything about do-it-yourself. Each consumer therefore has the potential to be an expert in one field or another. We all know a lot about something. And the internet helps to ensure that an increasing number of such expert consumers are able to have a growing influence on their environment. The average level of personal expertise

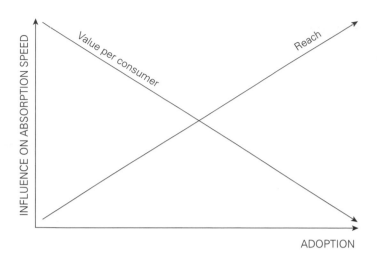

within our society is rising and so, consequently, is the total impact of the population on brands.

It is not only the 'experts' who help to build a brand. The fans also have their role to play. Fans promote your brand spontaneously and help to convince others of its merits. To be a fan of a brand means that your relationship with that brand goes further than the normal bond between customer and supplier. In fact, being a fan can sometimes mean that your feelings go much further, bordering on friendship or even infatuation.[141] Some consumers are happy to admit that they feel as if something is missing in their life if they do not have the opportunity to use their favourite brand on a regular basis.[142] This form of 'love' leads to a very strong commitment towards the brand. In the first instance, this kind of devotion might lead you to think of pop idols or football teams, but almost every type of product category is capable of inspiring this kind of tangible bond. Conversation Managers have great respect for their fans, and they actively cultivate their relationship with them. If fans are the first to receive new information about a brand, they feel appreciated by their 'friend', the brand holder, and will quickly proceed to engage others in conversation about the new buzz. For example, the way Universal Studios first informed its fans about the Harry Potter deal before the press is evidence of great fan respect – and this is the kind of respect that pays dividends.

Experts build brands by using their expertise within a particular domain. Fans build brands through their emotional bond with those

WDW Magic as a free travel agency

The website *WDWMagic.com* is a good example of how fans can build a brand. WDW stands for Walt Disney World. The fans of this fantastic theme park have developed this website to help tourists who are planning to head down Orlando way. The website contains everything you could ever possibly want to know about the Disney park: the menus in all the restaurants, a description of each attraction, visitor ratings, etc. The site also has its own much-visited forum, where the diehard fans can speculate about forthcoming innovations, whilst at the same time offering free and expert information to other routine site visitors. Fans who spontaneously take it upon themselves to provide this kind of high impact information to others are worth a lot of money to any brand. Disney understands this, too, and it is probably no coincidence that information about new attractions often finds its way more quickly onto these sites than onto other more official channels. Dries Tack, the marketing manager of Disneyland Paris, has put it like this: 'If I want to know about the forthcoming plans for our park, I find it easier to surf to one of the Disney fan sites. That way the news reaches me quicker than through our own internal channels of communication.'

brands. Both have important and influential profiles for a Conversation Manager. A frequently asked question in this context is: 'How do I track down these valuable people?' The answer is very simple: usually, they will find you! There are more of them and they are much closer than you might think. On your website, for example. A recent survey for a car manufacturer revealed that 80 per cent of the visitors to their website were already confirmed fans of the brand.[143] So don't worry, your fans will come to you. And much the same is true of experts: they are interested in what you do. For their different reasons, both categories will track you down.

Fans make fans: the success of Weight Watchers

The first meeting of Weight Watchers was held in the 1960s in the living room of Jean Nidetch, an American lady who was having a problem with those few extra pounds. Just two months later her group already had 40 members. Forty years later it has developed to become the epitome of healthy eating and healthy dieting. Today their programme has something like one and a half million active members worldwide, who meet together each week. In addition, there are countless others who maintain the Weight Watchers philosophy, but without attending meetings.

How can this phenomenal success be explained? Weight Watchers is a brand that hardly ever advertises. Instead, it simply grows through its fans. The philosophy could not be more basic: you go to the weekly meeting, where you listen to people talk about healthy eating. Social control certainly has a part to play, since each Weight Watcher is weighed during the meeting. The diet is simple, too, being based on an easy-to-use points system. You can eat whatever you like, as long as you don't exceed the specified number of points per day. This allows you to eat more than just salad and tomatoes, and makes it easier to stick to the diet over a longer period. The combination of a flexible and efficient product gives the members a good feeling. People are happy that they can lose weight in such a positive manner and so they tell their family and friends about it. 'I have already lost 5 kilos and I can still eat chocolate, as long as I stay within my daily points total. It couldn't be easier, and its fun too!' As a result of this philosophy, the million and a half Weight Watchers need little persuasion to go in search of new recruits – while the Weight Watchers organization needs to do virtually nothing!

Dimension 2. The right motivation encourages buying behaviour

Activation is only successful if the consumer spreads the brand message for the right reasons and in the right way. Harry Potter novels have become so successful because the fans have infected others with their enthusiasm. The motivation for their word-of-mouth was their high level of satisfaction with the books. By telling short scraps of the stories, they were able to excite the imagination of other people who had never even heard of them. During their next visit to a bookstore, these 'converts' went home with one or more Rowling books under their arm. In a similar fashion, students who encourage each other to watch *Temptation Island*, with the specific purpose of laughing at the candidates, actually increase the viewing figures to a significant degree in the short-term. However, this is not good brand activation, because the reason for the motivation will not increase overall brand identification in the long-run. In contrast, the T-Mobile film clip which was watched by 17 million people fitted perfectly with the brand's new slogan: this was positive activation. The Disney fans who created *WDWMagic.com* to encourage other consumers to visit Disneyworld is the best possible kind of activation, and will certainly boost Disney's already impressive profits.

The key influencers for activation are brand experience[144] and brand advertising.[145] Brand experience is unquestionably the biggest driver of activation. (Dis)satisfaction with a brand is a good predictor of the likely amount of word-of-mouth.[146] It is perhaps counter-intuitive that the amount of positive word-of-mouth is greater than the amount of negative comment. In fact, there is six times more positive WOM than negative (both online and offline). Moreover, positive wom is intrinsically more believable than negative.[147] For many marketeers the fear of negative feedback prevents them from seeking to promote meaningful activation. But this fear is ungrounded. If a brand has a good level of identification with its consumers, then the feedback can only be positive. Regularly giving people something new that they can talk about in relation to their experience of your brand is therefore of crucial importance.

The secondary driver of activation is brand advertising. One in every five conversations about brands is connected to advertising.[148] The advertisements are inevitably linked to the brand. A good example of how clever advertising can act as a driver for market activation is the Sony Bravia campaign. Some years ago, Sony launched a spot in which brightly coloured paint danced through the streets of New York, to the accompaniment of lively music. One in every six viewers felt activated on seeing this spot. Two-thirds of them spoke to others about its quality and one in every three actually spoke about the Sony Bravia.[149] The consumers who talked about the spot with others had a higher opinion of the quality of the spot than the people who did not feel activated. The activated consumers particularly appreciated the warm feeling which the spot gave them, combined with its high degree of originality.

What was supposed to be the most original Chevy advert ever...[150]

In March 2006 Chevrolet wanted to implement its own version of the activation philosophy with the launch of its new Sports Utility Vehicle (or SUV). They decided to do this by allowing consumers to design the advert. By involving the public in this manner, they hoped to encourage thousands of people to create a spot which would reflect the classic image of the SUV: namely, a large family vehicle, offering the benefits of a sporty car with plenty of luggage space.

What was the result? It was the environmental activists who wanted to stop the sale of the car (because of its high pollution levels) who were activated. Even Al Gore responded to Chevrolet's invitation to contribute. This was his message: *'This SUV gets just 12 miles to the gallon, and releases tons of carbon every year that will stay in the atmosphere for 100 years. Temperatures are rising, polar icecaps are melting, growing food is getting harder, violent storms are increasing, global warming is happening now. What will you tell your kids you drove?'*

The motivation of environmental activists is to secure greater world commitment against global warming – not to become famous for 15 minutes by participating in a car advert. This ambition hardly squares with what Chevrolet had hoped and with what the new SUV was promising. What was Chevy's ideal scenario? That fans would make positive word-of-mouth as a result of their strong brand loyalty and would warmly recommend the new SUV to other consumers. What actually happened? Their campaign was hijacked by people who spread negative word-of-mouth about their brand. This is a good example of the wrong way to try and secure consumer involvement in market activation. You cannot force people to go in a direction they don't want if your brand identification is inadequate.

Dimension 3. The right subject is essential

If a consumer circulates a mail about an advertisement with the comment: 'Just look how ridiculous this is', this is hardly likely to be a Conversation Manager's idea of how activation should work!

WHEN YOU KNOW THE SIGNS, YOU'RE GOING TO HAVE A GREAT NIGHT OUT. ENJOY HEINEKEN RESPONSIBLY.

The content of the conversation always determines whether or not the activation is likely to have an impact. For example, the tone of the message – is it positive or is it negative? – can make a world of difference. Focusing on the right subject is also crucial. The conversation must be about your company's brand or your company's products. If the 500,000 people who watched the video about the Domino's Pizza turnaround all continued to talk about the bad quality of the past rather than the new and exciting taste of the present, the message would have missed its target. If Chanel No.5 uses Nicole Kidman as its front woman, then they should not be surprised if people talk about 'that perfume with Kidman' rather than 'that exciting new fragrance from Chanel'.

In 2007 Goodyear tested two viral marketing campaigns.[151] At first glance, there seemed little to choose between the two. Market research yielded positive feedback for both versions. However, on further analysis, it became clear that there was one 'small' difference. In one of the spots, the conversations between the consumers were largely about humour. In the other spot, the conversations were less humorous, but were largely about Goodyear and the safety performance of their tyres. In this case, the Conversation Manager would always choose the second spot. Even though its activation potential is lower, its impact on the brand is likely to be greater.

This third dimension is your personal control factor. Check that you are not seeking to achieve activation without purpose. Knowing what consumers are likely to be saying after they have seen your advertising campaign has become an important element of pre-testing.

Molson's photo-competition goes badly wrong[152]

In this case, what was supposed to be a fun and positive activation campaign went badly wrong. The Molson beer brand asked university students to upload photos of their parties on the competition page on *Facebook*. The college which was chosen as the 'best party school in Canada' would win an all-expenses paid 8,000 dollar holiday to Mexico. Molson's aim was to increase their level of brand identification with young consumers and genuine brand fans.

The reaction of the universities was devastating. They insisted that Molson's should scrap the competition immediately, since it was encouraging irresponsible (ab)use of alcohol. Certain photos could also have a negative effect on students who would soon be looking for a job. Moreover, Molson' s attitude simply served to confirm the outmoded stereotype that all students are just drunken bums – at least according to the critics.

The campaign certainly achieved the desired level of activation, but not in the manner that was hoped for. The photos posted on *Facebook* – most of which could best be described as 'extreme' (and that's putting it lightly) – generated large numbers of conversations, but nearly all about the last subject that Molson's wanted to hear: irresponsible and unhealthy drinking. Molson's pulled the plug on the campaign after less than a month.[153]

A dream job on an uninhabited island[154]

The Queensland tourist department in Australia once advertised for a new employee who would be willing to 'maintain' an island on the Great Barrier Reef for a six-month period. The 'island caretaker' was asked to live rent-free for six months on an uninhabited island, in

Heineken campaigns against excessive use of alcohol[155]

Heineken wanted to become involved in the battle to combat excessive use of alcohol. For this type of campaign, it is common practice to show photographs of terrible traffic accidents, in the hope that this will persuade young people of the evils of drinking and driving. However, research has shown that this sort of campaign no longer leads to a change of behaviour. So Heineken decided to adopt a different approach.

In the autumn of 2008 Heineken started its 'know the signs' campaign. The campaign focused on different situations in which drunken people are likely to make a fool of themselves. There were images of aggressive drunks, exhibitionist drunks, amorous drunks, etc. The film clips on the campaign site were hilarious and (unfortunately for the participants) recognizable. It was an approach which appealed to young people and it created activation. By showing how people behave when they are drunk, these embarrassing films made the topics open for discussion.

Super-swimsuits

In July 2009 the swimming world championships were held in Rome. Conversations about the championships were dominated by talk of the new swimming suits used by many of the competitors. Brands such as Jaked and Arena launched swimming suits which significantly enhanced performance. There had never been so many world records at a single championships. It was embarrassing to see how swimmers who were sponsored by Speedo (including Michael Phelps) were forced to be highly 'economical with the truth' during press conferences in order not to bring their own sponsor into discredit. Some of them didn't even bother, and talked openly about Arena suits while the Speedo logo screamed loudly from their tracksuits. There was word-of-mouth for Speedo, but the content of the conversations was all wrong – and almost certainly led to worse rather than to better sales results.

---

return for which he (or she) would be paid the not inconsiderable sum of 150,000 dollars. All the caretaker had to do was to blog each day about his adventures on the idyllic island. It almost sounds too good to be true! In this way, Queensland hoped to increase the attractiveness of the region for tourists.

To find the ideal person, the tourist department asked interested candidates to submit a video about themselves, but in a manner which showed that they would be able to demonstrate appropriate enthusiasm for the region and its charms through blogs and other multi-media techniques.

The results of the campaign were truly impressive. Via *Twitter* the 'island caretaker' amassed no fewer than 127,000 followers. A BBC report was watched by an estimated 3.7 million people. The number of tourists heading off to Queensland rose by 20 per cent! The tourist department had a budget of 1.9 million dollars for this campaign, but it yielded a media value estimated at some 330 million dollars. Not surprisingly, it also won a batch of awards from the advertising and marketing world.

Why was the campaign so successful? Simply because all the conversations emphasized how great it was to spend a few months alone, surrounded by the wonders of nature. The blog posts, the videos and all the other content was focused on the core message: 'Queensland is a beautiful place, so come and see it.' And that is exactly what many people did.

Coke Zero: taste the difference?

Coke Zero was launched onto the market in 2006. It was Coca-Cola's biggest product launch in 22 years.[156] The new product was targeted at men who are interested in a healthy diet. Cola Light was seen as being too feminine for these machos; Coke Zero was designed to offer them an alternative. The launch campaign focused heavily on the taste of the new Coke Zero. This taste was compared with the classic taste of Coca-Cola. One of the adverts showed a group of classic-Coke marketeers, who wanted to take their Zero colleagues to court, because they had stolen the taste of the original.

This led to a worldwide debate about the respective tastes of classic Coke, Diet Coke and Coke Zero. Is there a real difference or not? I can even remember us conducting blind tastings in our office over lunch! A word-of-mouth tracker study[157] confirmed that we were not alone in our interest. During the launch period there was great commotion about the (possible) different tastes of the three drinks. The content of these conversations was devoted exclusively to the product. And all the dimensions of the activation process were present. In other words, it was a truly successful launch. Very tasty!

The Blair Witch Project: first time around

The original budget for the film *The Blair Witch Project* was just a paltry 20,000 dollars. After an upgrade of the sound and picture quality, the final budget panned out at just over 500,000 dollars.[158] A lot of money to you and me, but chicken-feed by Hollywood standards. In 1999 the film finally reached the cinemas, and the result was as spectacular as it was unexpected: the horror movie grossed an amazing 248 million dollars.[159] This is equivalent to an ROI of almost 5000%. *The Blair Witch Project* is still the record holder for the best return to cost ratio in the history of film.

This was one of the very first occasions when a product 'snowballed' in this manner as a result of positive online word-of-mouth.[160] The first viewers asked whether the film was actually played by actors. Or was it a real film of a group of real young people who experienced a terrifying night in a wood? This discussion was conducted online, which led to an increase in the number of positive 'reviews'. In particular, students flocked to the cinemas in droves to see for themselves what all the fuss was about. Slowly but surely, *The Blair Witch Project* climbed its way to the top of the box-office rankings. Many people across the world use these rankings to help them choose the films they want to see. And so the success continued to grow, and grow, and grow. Afterwards, when all the commotion had died down, mature reflection suggested that the film was maybe not that good, after all. It was even nominated for a Razzie Award as the worst film of the year. Not that the film's investors were all that bothered. They were laughing all the way to the bank...

Absolutely necessary: 'sticky criteria'

Even if all three of the dimensions have been well thought-out and included in your activation process, your central message must still be strong enough to be carried by your consumers. The Conversation Manager must therefore create a message which meets six specific criteria. These six 'sticky' criteria are based on research by Chip and Dan Heath.[161]

1 Simplicity
It is enough to sell a single idea to your consumers. If Goodyear tells people that its tyres are both sporty and safe, this is more difficult to process and transmit than a message which focuses on safety alone.

2 Surprise
The message must attract and hold the attention of the consumer in an innovative and counter-intuitive manner.

3 Concrete
Formulate as clearly as possible exactly what you want to say to the consumer. This can involve the use of all the different senses. An advert for medicine for sore throats which uses a circular saw as a symbol for throat pain is making a clear and concrete statement. Everyone will immediately understand what is meant.

4 Credible
Advertisers often use research material or experts to make their message seem credible. This is one way, but it is also possible to personalize credibility. Credibility is one of the reasons why Obama is now sitting in the White House. He didn't get there simply by using a mass of statistics.

5 Emotional
Let the consumers feel what you mean. If you want to stop teenagers from smoking, it is less effective to tell them that it is bad for their health than to tell them that it makes their breath stink when they are kissing.

6 Stories
Nobody remembers adverts; everybody remembers a good story. Right from our earliest years, we were told stories which

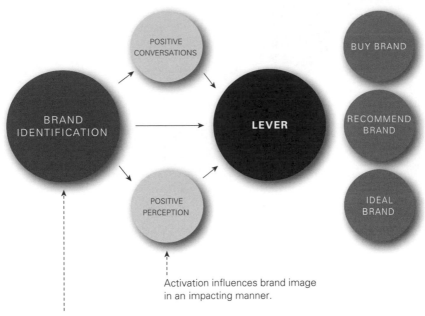

Activation influences brand image
in an impacting manner.

Brand identification increases if the consumer feels involved.
Activating consumers leads to high brand identification.

have remained with us for the rest of our lives. Remember this thought when you are communicating with your consumers. Try to keep them enthralled. The average classroom presentation by a student contains 2.5 statistics each minute, yet only one in ten attempts to tell a story. Yet if you ask the listening students what they remember from all these presentations, 63 per cent say that they remember the stories, whereas just 5 per cent remember the statistics.

Here is a brief test to prove our point. Do you remember John McCain's election slogan during the presidential campaign in 2008? If you ever knew it in the first place, the chance is small that you can remember it now. But what about Obama's slogan? Of course, everyone remembers that: '*Yes, we can!*' has gone down in American history, if not the history of the world. The message, and the way it was transmitted, corresponds perfectly to the six 'sticky' criteria listed above. Obama's message of hope was both credible and emotional. His story was inspirational and appealing: more than 300,000

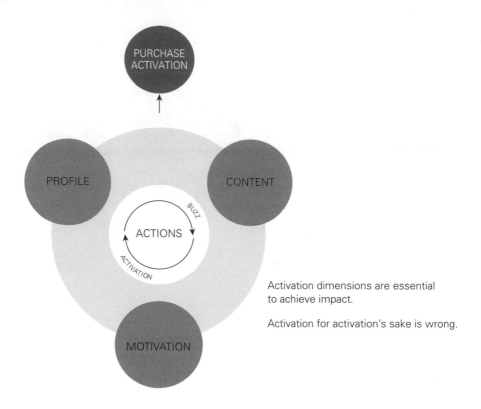

Activation dimensions are essential to achieve impact.

Activation for activation's sake is wrong.

people crowed onto the streets of Berlin to hear him talk. And the short but forceful '*Yes, we can!*' is concrete, simple and reflects his countrymen's belief in the American dream.

Campaign for real beauty by Dove: a classic example of activation[162]

For the jubilee congress of the European market research society Esomar in Berlin (2007) InSites Consulting analysed Dove's 'Evolution' campaign in detail, using the principles of the Conversation Manager. The objectives and set-up of this campaign have already been described in the first chapter of this book. Now we will attempt to explain the campaign's great success with reference to the Conversation Manager philosophy.

In reality, this explanation is simple: the campaign owed its success to perfect activation. A third of the consumers engaged in

word-of-mouth about 'Evolution'. They did this either by spreading the film or by discussing its message with their friends. This not only ensured that many people had direct contact with the message, but also that many more heard about it indirectly. Twenty-four per cent of young girls had actually seen the film themselves, while a further 12 per cent said that they had heard about it. In other words, the word-of-mouth increased the campaign's initial reach by 50 per cent (36 per cent instead of 24 per cent). The campaign encouraged mothers to talk with their daughters about the ideal of beauty and to make them aware of the impact that media could have on them. Nine out of every ten of these conversations was related to the message of the campaign. Research also showed that the level of activation was the same for fathers as for mothers. Fathers found it even more important than mothers to discuss the specific message of the film with their daughters. All dimensions of the activation model had been successfully triggered: concerned parents (dimension 1) wanted to talk to their daughters about the message of the film (dimension 3), in order to improve their self-image (dimension 2).

Similarly, testing the campaign against the six 'sticky' criteria reveals that these criteria were also met in full. The message was simple:

media distort our ideas about beauty. This was an idea that most people had no difficulty in believing. It was also made more concrete by giving an 'ordinary' woman a new hairstyle and new make-up. The unexpected element came in the Photoshop treatment given to the picture of the woman, transforming her into a beautiful fashion model. The message plays on our own concept of our self-image and that of our children. This tugs at the necessary emotional strings. Finally, the message was told by means of a story. Once you had seen the film, you were unlikely to forget it.

The Conversation Manager and advertising

While mass media may have made traditional advertisers lazy, advertising is a serious and time-consuming business for the Conversation Manager. Sending your message to the waiting world has become more complex than ever in recent decades. The Conversation Manager takes account of the modern consumer. He wants to use this consumer as a lever for his brand and hopes to encourage him to spread the message contained in his advertisements in a positive way.

Reach is the traditional measure for success. Reach is also important to the Conversation Manager, but to this he adds a new success criterion: the creation and spread of more messages. The impact of his advertising actions on his brand is central to his philosophy. A viral campaign which fails to actively support the brand or promote its identity is a failure, even if it has been seen by more than a million people. What people do is more important than who does it. The Conversation Manager also makes sure that consumers have something to talk about. An advertisement is not an end point, but rather a starting point for a conversation. What people say after they have seen the campaign forms the core of the preparation for further campaigns. The Conversation Manager tests each campaign against the six 'sticky' factors. If the message fails to reflect one of these factors, the story is much less likely to catch on with consumers.

THE KEY POINTS IN THIS CHAPTER

- The main objective of the Conversation Manager is *to use advertising to activate people:* in other words, to convince the target group to spread the brand message within their network and, in some cases, even to create new content themselves. *The hidden danger is activation for activation's sake.* The Conversation Manager wants to activate people with the intention of boosting his brand's marketing and sales figures. Campaigns with a high level of viral impact, but which focus on the campaign itself rather than on the brand, should be avoided at all costs.

- Activation is only successful if it combines the three key dimensions:

  1 the *'right' consumers* must spread the message

  2 thcy must have the *right reasons* for doing so

  3 they must talk about the *right subject*, ie the product or brand, and not the campaign itself.

  Only if all three of these dimensions can be triggered will activation actually contribute to a stronger brand.

- In order to spread your advertising effectively, your message will need to be 'sticky'. It must have a story which will lodge easily in the consumer's memory. You can do this by making your story emotional, credible, surprising, simple and concrete. Your message will be much easier for the consumer to remember and to pass on if you tell it in this story-like manner. Nobody remembers statistics.

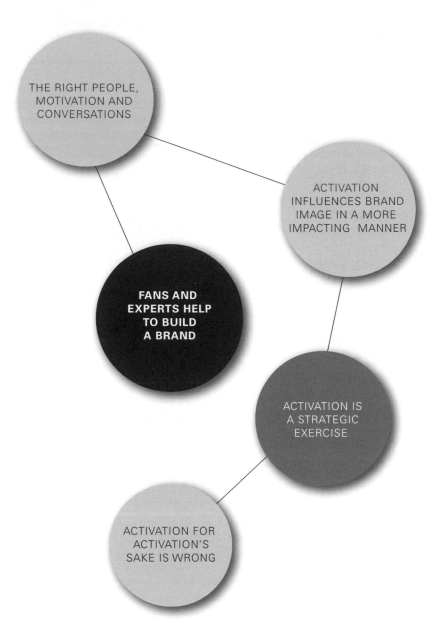

Chapter Six
Observe, facilitate and participate in conversations

Managing conversations: how?

Little has so far been written about how to manage conversations. And the little that has been written has been couched in very vague terms. Nevertheless, this is a subject of major importance for today's companies, struggling to survive in an increasingly complex world. Marketeers are aware of the opportunities which talking to consumers has to offer, but they are uncertain how to go about it.

To meet this challenge, there are a number of things you need to know. Firstly, the modern consumer is prone to expressive behaviour. More than ever, they like to talk about brands. Even better, they like to talk to companies. Their input is positive. They want to make a contribution towards successful products and they want to give feedback about their brand experience. As soon as the consumer is given the chance to participate in the marketing of 'their' brand, they expect in return that the products will become more 'personalized' to reflect their needs.[163] Above all, consumers want to be listened to. The conversation intensity is high. Their expectations of companies are clear.

Secondly, it is important to realize that brands and consumers are both capable of starting a conversation. The discussions which rage in the online discussion fora, the after-dinner chat at family get-togethers, telephone calls or e-mails from members of the public, consumers who contact the companies direct: these are all forms of conversation in which consumers can initiate talk about brands. Examples of conversations initiated by the brand holder may include: approaching smaller groups of consumers by asking them a question in a forum; organizing a competition for loyal customers; broadcasting an advert in the media. The philosophy of the Conversation Manager with regard to advertising fits in perfectly with this strategy. Advertising is the opening of a conversation with the consumers, but on a massive scale. In order to be a good conversation partner for consumers, it is important that the brand should initiate some discussions, but should also allow consumers to initiate some of their own. Balance rather than one-sidedness is the key. If you find that it is always the consumers who are taking the initiative, you are underusing your conversation management possibilities.

Thirdly – and most importantly – it is vital to know exactly what we mean by 'a conversation'. This is my definition: a conversation is an interaction which involves both talking and listening. Within a conversation, everyone has the same possibility to express his or her opinion. But learning to listen is something new – at least for advertisers. Conversation Management requires that you approach these conversations with and between consumers with an open mind. But the talent that you will undoubtedly most need to hone, practice and refine is... listening!

These three basic starting points will form the foundation for your ability to manage conversations. The most frequently asked question in workshops about conversation management is: 'How do we take part in conversations with consumers?' I normally answer this question with another question. 'How long have you already been observing the conversations of your customers?' This usually results in silence. After a few seconds they admit that they have never observed their customers' conversations! This is a fundamental mistake. Managing conversations begins with the observation and analysis of the things that consumers are talking about today. The main purpose of this is to acquire an understanding of the language used by consumers, to learn how they talk about your brand.

The next step is to think how you can facilitate these conversations, lend them a helping hand in the direction you want. It is useful to have a number of tools at your disposal which will allow you to converse efficiently with your consumers. A frequently cited example is the setting up of a customer community. This community makes it easy for people to talk about your brand. Because they return time after time to this site, their loyalty and commitment to your brand increases. For example, brands which sell kitchen equipment can set up a community which encourages people to exchange recipes. In short, as the brand holder you simply help people to come into contact with each other, so that they can share their experiences about your brand.

It is only in a final stage that you actually engage in conversation with your own consumers. Once you have built up your brand community, you have an ideal platform to ask questions or give answers. But when you talk to customers you should talk to them person-to-person, not as a representative of 'the brand'. Consumers hate impersonal standard messages: they want to talk to a real person, who will listen to their feedback and do something with it.[164]

We can therefore summarize the methodology of the Conversation Manager as follows: he observes conversations as a manager, he facilitates conversations as a brand and he takes part in conversations as himself. These are the three steps to managing conversations, each demanding a very different approach, if you wish to be successful. The biggest mistake of all is to take part in a conversation as a manager. Consumers will quickly be put off by management jargon and statistics, so that all your best efforts will have the opposite effect.

In the rest of this chapter we will be looking at each of the three steps individually.

Observe: learn to walk before you run

Question 1. Do you regularly search for online conversations about your brand?

Question 2. Have you ever searched *Google* for your brand name?

We have asked hundreds of workshop participants these questions during the past three years, and so I know that the percentage of 'yes' answers to question 1 is somewhere between 10 per cent and 15 per cent. The percentage of 'yes' answers to question 2 is around 95 per cent. The painful conclusion of this brief exercise is that advertisers are busier following themselves on the web than following their brand.

The Conversation Manager understands the importance of conversations between consumers. He organizes himself and his team in such a way that they are constantly able to absorb this flow of incoming information. He regards listening to these conversations as a kind of safari. Perhaps, after hours of trekking through the jungle, he will find nothing at all. But the following morning he might stumble across a herd of elephants or a pride of lions. This is the price that you have to pay if you want to observe conversations correctly. One day you will find little of interest in your consumers' chit-chat, but the next day you might hear something new and exciting, which may lead to your next product idea.

The Conversation Manager's approach to observation is all-embracing. He observes always and everywhere. During every family party, during every visit to the pub, during every football match conversations about brands are taking place. This means that the motto of the Conversation Manager must be: 'Keep your eyes and ears open!' When the Garasil vaccine against cervical cancer was launched onto the market at the beginning of 2008 it was a major topic of conversation amongst women. It was discussed with friends and colleagues, at home and in the office. This provided an ideal opportunity to learn more about the market. It wasn't necessary to intervene in these conversations. It was only necessary to listen to what these women had to say, and how they said it, the words that they used, the questions that they asked. For a pharmaceutical marketeer, this was a treasure trove of information! In other words, the world is a never-ending voyage of discovery. Once you approach it in this manner, every time you step outside your front door you are embarking on

So You Think You Can Dance?: better television each week

The programme concept *So You Think You Can Dance* has been a TV-hit in several countries. In the autumn of 2008, the RTL 5 channel first broadcast the programme in The Netherlands. Using a series of auditions, boot-camps and live shows, RTL went in search of Holland's new dance sensation. The winner was duly rewarded with a prestigious dance-training abroad, pocket money of 20,000 euros and a solo act in the new dance musical *Footloose*. In order to learn more about reaction to their live shows, RTL decided to monitor the online conversations of viewers over a number of weeks. They were particularly interested in the opinions of the watching public about the different component elements of the programme: presentation (eg camera work), content (eg different dance styles), the jury, the hosts, voting behaviour, etc. They reasoned that if they discovered something interesting, they could quickly include it in (or remove it from) the following show. An analysis was made of different communication channels and websites. The opinions of the RTL forum were then compared with the opinions of other social media. On the one hand, this allowed the programme-makers to assess whether or not their website was capable of absorbing and responding to the commotion created by the programme, and on the other hand whether or not the content of the site compared with the content of the other sources.

a journey into the unknown. But it is a journey that can enrich your knowledge and your understanding. Even observing conversations about other brands from other sectors is a useful way to learn more about how consumers think and feel. We have already mentioned that mass media has made advertisers lazy. In contrast, the Conversation Manager needs to stand with both feet firmly on the ground. The consumer needs to be rediscovered.

In addition to this 'field' work, the Conversation Manager must also regularly follow consumer conversations on the internet. The intensity of these conversations reflects the current consumer importance of your brand. The information that the Conversation Manager is looking for is the same as in his offline searches: the questions people ask, the words they use, the arguments which seem credible. All these things teach the Conversation Manager the techniques which he will need to use when he intervenes in these conversations at a later stage. But this is something which will only be possible after listening long and hard to consumer dialogues. A baby listens for a year and a half to its parents before it says its first word. Much the same should be true for an advertiser. It is impossible to converse in a natural manner if you are not conversant with the language of your conversation partner. In Chapter 8 (The Conversation Manager's toolbox) we will be looking at a number of free online tools that can help you.

It is essential that the Conversation Manager should go in search of interesting consumer conversations, but by itself this is not enough. In order to take good management decisions, it is necessary to have a more total insight. It is impossible to do this manually and so the Conversation Manager makes use of software which can extract conversations from the internet on a large scale. These conversations are downloaded into a database, where they can be analysed statistically. This information will give you a list of subjects for attention in order of consumer priority. It will also provide you with a number of qualitative insights. By linking particular emotions (sad, angry, afraid) to particular words, you will learn far more about consumers than by simply counting the number of people who are talking about a specific topic. The Conversation Manager needs to have a good understanding of the relationship between words. Which words and phrases are used most often in association with your brand? What feelings are coupled to the use of these words? This is the only way to gain deep and meaningful insights into the conversations which people conduct on the internet. And these insights will help you to optimize existing products and services, and provide possible ideas for new ones. Ideas lead to new products based on the unfulfilled expectations and needs of consumers. Hans Schmeits, vice-president of global marketing services for the pharmaceutical company UCB, once described consumer observation in the following terms: 'It offers me answers to the questions I don't yet have.'

100 Calories

The following example relating to the Kraft Corporation is a good example of the positive results that can flow from good observation. By watching and listening to its consumers, Kraft discovered that many of them had difficulty working out the number of calories contained in the foods they were eating. Food packaging at this time was traditionally labelled in xxx grams, whereas the number of calories was detailed per 100 grams. For someone in the middle of a diet, this is not the most user-friendly way to receive this information. This became apparent from an analysis of online fora in which foodstuffs and dieting were discussed. The findings were confirmed by Professor Wansink in his 'food & brand lab' at Cornell University.[165] A further conclusion was that consumers are interested in keeping an eye on what they are eating, but are not prepared to make a major effort to achieve it. In other words, they want to be taken by the hand and shown the best and easiest way to eat healthily. On the basis of all these observations, plus a number of other external insights, Kraft decided to develop the '100 Calorie Pack'. During the first six months following the product launch on the American market, turnover amounted to 75 million dollars. Kraft announced growth of 27 per cent during the first quarter of 2005, in comparison with 2004.[166] This growth was largely attributable to the effects of the launch. A good observation strategy had led to the creation of a new product, the 100 Calorie Pack. And this in turn had lead to the strong growth of Kraft as a company.

The Conversation Manager can obtain new insights simply by observing others. He can then check these insights against scientific research. If the research results confirm his findings, he may have the seeds of a major success on his hands.

Help! My company has jammed Facebook!

About 50 per cent of companies ban the use of *Facebook* on the work floor.[167] The number of companies that effectively jam *Facebook* has doubled in the last 12 months. The official line is that companies jam social network sites to avoid the risk of viruses. In reality, they are worried about the productivity of their staff. In 1999 there was a similar fuss about e-mails. Companies were afraid that this new medium would allow confidential documents to be transferred to rival organizations. Worse still, you could actually send people personal messages during working hours! The very idea! No doubt in a more distant past similar discussions were held about coffee and cigarette-breaks. The management's point is this: employers are expected to show responsibility and to carry out their duties to the best of their abilities. This is very true, as most people would agree.

But the counter argument is this: a good employee is unlikely to become a bad one, simply because he/she has access to *Facebook*. Admittedly, a bad employee might have one more toy to play with, but this is a problem of recruitment and training – it is not the fault of *Facebook*.

The Conversation Manager needs optimal access to the internet. Observing consumers without access to social network sites is simply not possible. A top manager in a major company recently told me that he had blocked *Facebook* for the whole company. Staff in the marketing and communications departments had the possibility to unblock it, and this on the face of it was a wise management decision. More disquieting, however, was the fact that only one member of staff made use of this option. For a modern advertiser, marketeer or communications manager, searching for information about your brand on the web has become an integral part of their job. You may have no personal interest in what is being said on social network sites, but you are being paid to understand consumers. On the basis of this understanding, you are expected to communicate with them. But this is impossible if you do not understand their language. And you learn this language by constant observation. And where can you best do this observing? On social networks like *Facebook*!

David Meerman Scott[168] recommends taking things even a step further. He advises advertisers to try and persuade their customers of the added value of these sites in terms of marketing policy. Maybe you should try the same line with your employers. If they refuse to accept the argument, perhaps you might be better advised to look for another job. The future of your present company isn't looking too bright.

Facilitate: welcome consumers with open arms

The second phase in conversation management is something of a leap in the dark for most companies. Facilitating discussions means offering a platform where consumers are given the chance to converse with each other (and later with your brand). The Conversation Manager succeeds in encouraging a group of consumers to talk freely about their brand experiences. He does not take an active part in these conversations (yet). The platform for discussion can either be online or offline. The ideal scenario is a combination of both. In this respect, it is wise to pretend that there is no boundary between online and offline in terms of promoting consumer conversations. Supporters of Liverpool FC are active daily in discussion groups about the club (online). At weekends, they continue these discussions face-to-face on the terraces (offline). Cooking magazines which have an online forum for the exchange of consumer recipes, the best of which are then published in the magazine, is another good example of the way online and offline can go hand in hand.

Companies are wary of a business model founded on such communities. The fight between economic and social elements is an important battle for the future of our business success. And it is a battle that has long been predicted.[169] Communities of this kind are not created to have a direct impact on the company's financial results. A community serves to offer added value to its users.[170] The beneficial result of a community can only be felt indirectly in the short term. But there are unquestionably benefits for the development of your brand in the long term. Brand identification leads to positive conversations and to better brand perception. Above all, it helps to create a lever effect that gives a positive boost to the sales figures of the brand. In this sense, facilitation has a double purpose: to acquire insights into the useful conversations of your consumers and to bind them ever more tightly to your brand.

Apart from the financial aspect (the setting up of a community requires a substantial investment), many companies refuse to take this step out of fear. This type of platform is usually developed as an online community, where consumers can talk freely about their brand experiences. This means that their comments can either be positive or negative. They may even end up talking about your competitors. This possibility makes traditional advertisers uneasy.

And in some ways they have a point. What they fear will almost certainly happen. (In fact, I can guarantee it!) But does this necessarily have to be a bad thing. Absolutely not! What does a Liverpool fan do if an Arsenal fan suddenly starts getting involved in a discussion on the Liverpool site? What you would expect: he defends his favourite team tooth and nail. Without the presence of such outside 'invaders', a negative story about the club may occasionally appear, but once the 'enemy' has been sighted, the faithful close ranks and support their brand – fanatically, if need be. And it is not too far-fetched to imagine that the same sort of thing could happen within the Apple community, if a group of Nokia fans try to rubbish the iPhone. A Jamie Oliver forum would no doubt have both supporters and opponents of his recipes. But this, I repeat, is not bad. In fact, it is essential that rivals appear from time to time in your brand community. A common enemy is the best possible stimulation for brand identification.

Finally, companies also hesitate to set up a community because of the cost and effort of managing it. But this is missing the point. You don't have to control or manipulate your community. All you need to do in the first instance is to observe it. If you are tempted to censure any of the negative messages which may appear, your community will not last very long. One of our pharmaceutical clients once wanted to set up a community, where patients would be able to share their experiences of a particular sickness. A good idea, in theory, were it not for the fact that every patient first had to pass a 'controller' before his or her message could be posted on the site. This also led to a delay of 48 hours before the messages finally appeared. After a month, there were just 20 messages: the good idea had been suffocated because of the company's excessive desire to control. Facilitating a conversation means offering a platform for open discussion. It does not mean doing everything you can to push the conversation in the direction you want it to go. There are no scenarios for this kind of conversation. That is why it scares the traditional advertiser. And that is why a Conversation Manager sees it as an opportunity.

FC Bruges learns from its online community

When FC Bruges recorded a series of poor results in 2006, a number of the fans became dissatisfied. What every manager fears, now actually happened. On the forum on the club website *clubbrugge.be* a furious discussion broke out. The chief target of the fans' displeasure was the board of directors. The use of language on the forum became heated, almost offensive. And so the club took a drastic decision: the forum was temporarily shut down.

Yunomi, the female community of Unilever[171]

Yunomi is an online community which focuses on women between 30 and 50 years of age. The site seeks to cater to female needs by offering them 'time to be themselves'. It is the intention that women should participate actively in the site. For example, they can tell their own story in the section entitled 'Woman of the Day'. Via 'My Yunomi' members can save their favourite articles and recipes. Every visit to the website allows them to save 'Nomi's', savings points which they can exchange at the end of each quarter for a nice present. In addition, every day during the month of June Yunomi fans have the chance to win a special Indulgence Day, with prizes such as a private dance lesson, a photo-workshop in their own house or personal lingerie advice. Ivonne Boumeester, manager of Consumer Relationships at Unilever Benelux says: 'Through the combination of home, work and family, women often feel the need for more time to themselves. Yunomi hopes to offer these women a few moments of calm and personal reflection in the course of a busy day. Yunomi also helps Unilever to fulfil its "vitality mission" – our wish to help people look better, feel better and get more out of life. In addition, the new online platform allows Unilever to build up a long-term, mutual relationship with this important consumer group. This fits in perfectly with our strategy of further developing our relational marketing.'

Such a decision is not without risk. Regular visitors to the forum were effectively having their mouths sealed shut. If someone is given an opportunity to express an opinion, but then has that opportunity unilaterally taken away from him, it is reasonable to assume that he will become even angrier. Closing down a forum can only lead to positive results in very extreme circumstances. And this was proven to be the case now. FC Bruges had not solved its problem: it had simply shifted it elsewhere. A new community quickly established itself on the site *blue-army.com*. This website was managed by the supporters' association – and was therefore beyond the control of the club management. The negative discussion continued... After a time, things quietened down, but the forum has never reappeared on the official club website. This is also a lesson worth noting: once you shut down a forum, it is almost impossible to revive it. The mutual confidence on which it was based has been destroyed.

The club management eventually sat around the table with the committee of the supporters' association. They all agreed that this type of communication was not doing the club any favours. The Blue Army committee undertook to tackle the problem – and their solution was to act as listening ear to the supporters. They would then serve as a bridge between the supporters and the club, passing on information as necessary. Notwithstanding the continuing poor results in the seasons that followed, the tone of the fans' comments has never been as negative as it was in 2006. This suggests that closing down a forum is not the answer. That is the strategy of fear – and fear is always a bad guide to policy. Allowing people to vent their feelings in a forum, allowing them to 'get it off their chest', can often have a therapeutic effect. That is the strategy of the Conversation Manager.

Facilitating conversations for the launch of the Ford Fiesta[172]

In 2011 Ford plans to launch its Fiesta model on the American market. In order to convince this market that small cars can also be 'cool', Ford has chosen to mount an innovative launch campaign.

The company invited 100 people to drive for a number of weeks with the car, and then share their experiences with other consumers via different social media. These 100 guinea pigs were selected from more than 4,000 applicants. They were just ordinary Americans, with no previous background of opinion-forming in the motor industry. Some outsiders thought that Ford was taking a big risk, since it was allowing just 100 consumers to form the public perception of their product. Even so, it is a perfect example of how you can use your brand to facilitate and stimulate conversations. In the final analysis, the image of the car will always be determined by public feedback, so you might as well facilitate that feedback yourself. Ford put no pressure on its test-drivers to reach specific conclusions: it was happy to accept their honest opinions. These honest opinions – and the real experiences on which they are based – are now starting to appear on the net. Even if there are one or two technical problems with the cars, this does not necessarily have to be a bad thing for Ford. They way in which they deal with their problems can be a new opportunity to convince people of the credibility of the brand.

Six months after the start of the action, the results are excellent. More than 4 million people have seen at least one *YouTube* film about the Fiesta, made by one of the hundred testers. More than 500,000 people have seen photographs of the new model on *Flickr*. *Twitter* has registered some 3 million messages about the campaign. Perhaps most importantly, Ford has already had 50,000 pre-launch orders for the new Fiesta (97 per cent from people who are not currently Ford owners). These are impressive results – particularly if you remember that they all come from just 100 people driving around for a few weeks in the same car!

Participate: be yourself

'Markets want to talk with companies,' announced *The Cluetrain Manifesto*[173] in 2000. These were prophetic words. The authors were already describing how markets were made from conversations between people. These people want to (and are able to) make their opinions known to companies. Companies which have the talent to enter into a dialogue with their consumers will be the successful marketing companies of the 21st century.

After a period of observing and facilitating, the Conversation Manager has the necessary input to enter into this dialogue. Knowing which words consumers use to describe your market is essential. It is of great importance to talk to consumers naturally, in a language they can understand. In no circumstance must the consumer feel that he is being talked to (and certainly not talked down to) by a big, impersonal company. The consumer wants to feel that he is talking to another ordinary person, someone who is prepared to listen and can give meaningful answers to his questions, someone who asks questions in return and seems to understand what the consumer is thinking and feeling. The use of language in these conversations cannot be compared with any other type of communication currently used in the business world. Advertisers are trained to write perfectly crafted texts for websites, brochures and press releases. But the language they use sounds distant and official. This must always be avoided in a conversation with a consumer.

A conversation with a consumer is based on six principles:

1 **Listen**

If a consumer starts a conversation with you, focus your attention clearly on what that person has to say. A consumer can approach you through a number of different channels (e-mail, face-to-face, in a community, etc). Whichever channel he uses, if he has taken the trouble to contact you, it means that it is important to him. You must therefore listen to him patiently and attentively, even if he is saying negative things about your brand.

2 **Ask questions**

In order to understand the consumer properly, it may be necessary to ask a number of questions. Perhaps your first instinct is to counter-attack, by showing him the weaknesses in his arguments. This is a bad move, which only leads to frustration, and does nothing to solve the problem. By asking questions, the consumer will feel that you are showing genuine interest. You also help him to provide a more appropriate framework for his own arguments. Always make yourself ask at least five additional, open questions in every conversation with a consumer. Good questions include: 'What do you mean exactly?', 'Can you give me an example of that?', 'How do you see your idea in concrete terms?'

3 Adopt an open-minded attitude

A consumer may bring you a good idea, but sometimes at first you only see the practical problems which make it difficult to implement. But perhaps you were not listening closely enough. Go back and think about it again. Many successful commercial opportunities are created from suggestions generated by the market. Be open to the ideas of your consumers.

4 Be honest

If a conversation between an advertiser and a consumer does not reach a successful conclusion, this is nearly always because the advertiser has lied. A consumer has an inborn talent for sniffing out lies about his favourite brand. So be honest! If there is a problem with one of your products, tell this to the consumer quickly and clearly.

5 Be a person

Conversations with consumers are not something you can contract out to an advertising bureau. A consumer wants to talk with a representative of 'his' brand, and not with someone hired from outside. Speak in your own name as person X, employed by brand Y. Never speak 'on behalf of' brand Y. This is too impersonal.

6 Commit yourself

A good conversation often leads to action. Assure your consumers that their input will be used. If possible, show them at a later stage what has been done with this input. Make it a rule to use a number of ideas each year which have come from your consumers.

We use these six criteria naturally, if we want to have a good conversation with our family, friends or colleagues. It therefore makes sense to use this same approach if we want to talk meaningfully to consumers. This is what the consumer expects, and it deepens his attachment to your brand. Equally important, always have a positive attitude towards your conversations and your conversation partners. Consumers are put at ease by a friendly, positive tone of voice. Finally, always remember to personally thank consumers who strengthen your brand by their word-of-mouth.

These criteria are by no means new or unique, but their systematic application in marketing is truly innovative. 'Building a brand together'

is one of the Conversation Manager's strongest convictions, a key part of his marketing strategy. But this is only possible by talking to your consumers.

Lies never pay: the story of Kryptonite

On 12 September 2004 a blog message appeared on the site *bikeforums.net*.[174] The message described how you could easily break open the Kryptonite bike-lock with a ballpoint pen. At this time, the *bikeforums.net* website had an average of 11,000 visitors per day. The following day, a consumer placed a video on the site which confirmed that the previous day's message was true. On 14 September the number of site visitors shot up to 180,000. A day later a staggering 900,000 people logged on to have a look at the film.

The company management was aware of this turbulence in its online community. They launched a press release which denied the claim in the strongest possible terms. The public were assured that this was an isolated case, rather than a structural problem.

The press release landed on the desk of journalist Lydia Polgreen at the *New York Times*. She decided to do a test.[175] She went down to her local bike store and bought one of the more expensive Kryptonite locks. Within 30 seconds, she had managed to open it. The Kryptonite press release worked like red rag to a bull. Polgreen decided to write an article about Kryptonite's 'economy with the truth'. Her article appeared on 17 September on an inside page in the *NYT*. On 19 September the number of visitors on *bikeforums.net* reached 1.8 million (in comparison with 11,000 just five days previously). On 22 September Kryptonite issued a new press release, this time announcing that all the defective locks would be replaced free of charge. The estimate cost? Ten million dollars.

What lessons can be learnt from this sorry tale? It might be stating the obvious, but it must always be remembered that we are living in an era of zero-tolerance as far as product defects are concerned. If something is wrong with a product, the consumers will soon get to know about it and they will not be afraid to tell others. It is also a given that lying about a product's defects will always have a boomerang effect on the company. When Kryptonite launched its first reassuring press release, things quietened down a little on *bikeforums.net*. But when the real truth became known, consumer reaction was twice as fierce. Kryptonite was playing with fire – and, as a result, got its fingers burnt.

Conclusion: listen to consumers and discuss problems with them. Don't try to cover up mistakes or faults. Be honest in your communication. Lying to the public never pays – not in this day and age.

From Dell to Hell, and back[176]

Dell is a success story. The company was founded in the 1980s by Michael Dell. Growth was rapid and by 2002 Dell was recognized as one of the world's leading players in the personal computer market.

In June 2005 Jeff Jarvis, a media consultant and blogger, bought a Dell computer with a four-year guarantee. This guarantee promised to repair the computer, if any problems arose. Which is precisely what happened with Jarvis: after a few weeks, his computer was no longer working. When he contacted Dell, they told him to send the computer back: the repairs service was unable to carry out this particular repair

Gertje, haven't you forgotten something?

Studio 100 is one of the trendsetting companies in Europe for children's entertainment. The company operated initially in Belgium, but now manages a number of internationally-known programmes and cartoon books, such as *Bumba, Pippi Longstocking*, etc.

At the beginning of 2007, a Flemish student started a tongue-in-cheek action against the boss of Studio 100, Gert Verhulst – Gertje for short. Via a website[177] he sent the following message, under the title: 'Gertje, haven't you forgotten something?'

Gert Verhulst, you might have forgotten, but we haven't! Back in 1991 (now some 16 years ago!) you promised us a party, litres of lemonade and a hundred kilos of chocolate. You told us that if you had 10 million [the title of a song by Gert and Samson, a television puppet dog] we could all come along and join in. The 1991 generation is now all grown up, but we still wouldn't mind the party, the litres of lemonade and (above all) the hundred kilos of chocolate. We know that you wrote these lyrics a long time ago – no doubt meaning every word – but we think that the time has now come to give us our due reward. We have waited long enough, and we all know that you now have 10 million – at least! Promises are made to be kept, Gert Verhulst!

We will use the pages of this website to build up our weight of evidence against the accused, Gert Verhulst. But we are sure that this won't be necessary! As a peace-loving and civilized generation, we are happy to offer Gert an alternative solution: Let's Party!

This site soon attracted the sympathy of a large public. The newspapers picked up the story and gave it national coverage. The solution which the student suggested to Gert Verhulst was to make Plopsa Indoor (an indoor theme park for toddlers, based on another Studio 100 programme) available to the student and his friends for their party.

A few days later, the following message was posted on the website:

We did it! The party is on!
The tickets have already been sent – and what a stampede it was! Almost in the twinkling of an eye, the thousand available tickets were snapped up. Time now for me to look back on the whole stunt and to thank people for spreading the link. Without you, we never could have done it! This website, started as a joke, has achieved far more than I ever dared to hope. The tickets for the lucky thousand sadly mean that I have had to disappoint many others. However, Plopsa Indoor is limited in terms of its capacity and Studio 100 has – quite rightly – given a chance to 500 other less fortunate people to take part in our party. And so there remains little more for me to say, other than to repeat: 'We did it!' During the next few weeks I will try to update the website

> with the most fun reactions... My apologies to all those who won't be able to be there. But I am sure you understand the way things are!
>
> This is a brilliant example of what can be achieved by a conversation. One consumer poses a question to a company in public. The company has a choice: it can ignore the question, and laugh it off as a joke. Or it can respond positively to the question, working with the consumer to achieve something of benefit to both of them. Studio 100 wisely chose the second option. The goodwill which it was able to create by allowing the party to take place was far greater than anything which traditional advertising could have achieved. This is perfect Conversation Management. And there was also an interesting follow-up to this story: a year later the student graduated, and he now works as... a PR-manager for Studio 100!

in his home. Jarvis was so angry at what he saw as a complete lack of customer service that he described his experiences and his emotions on his blog. He received 253 reactions in his blog mail from people who had experienced the same thing. Jarvis kept in touch with these people, and others who soon joined in the debate, and gradually the term 'Dell Hell' emerged to describe the company's lack of concern for its consumers. Thousands of bloggers were quick to adopt this term. In the meantime, a study was published by the University of Michigan which showed that consumer satisfaction with Dell had fallen dramatically in just 12 months time. The main reason for this failing confidence was the poor quality of the after-sales service. Blog research indicated that 60 per cent of all online conversations about Dell were negative.

Bad news, indeed – but within a year Dell had repaired the reputation of its brand. The company set up two communication initiatives which made use of social media. To begin with, Dell launched its own blog in June 2006: *Direct2Dell*. This allowed customers to send feedback directly to the company, which in turn allowed the company to react more quickly to problems connected with its customer-relations service. Dell also recruited a team of Dell 'advocates', who were specially trained to deal with the online comments and concerns of Dell consumers (see box, page 142). A year after the introduction of this platform the proportion of negative comments had fallen to just 23 per cent.

The second Dell initiative was launched in February 2007: *IdeaStorm*, an online platform where consumers could submit their ideas for the improvement of Dell products. The Dell service and product development team used this site as a source of inspiration for new products and new services, working in close collaboration with the Dell fans.

By failing to listen to its consumers, Dell had put its strong reputation at risk. By learning to listen again to its consumers, and by working together with them, the company restored and even improved its position. Surely the moral of the story is clear?

Is an answer always necessary?

Does participating in a conversation mean that you always have to react to what consumers say? Of course it doesn't!

Sometimes, silence is golden. Here are a number of examples where it is advisable simply to observe, rather than to take active part.

1 **Emotional reactions**
   If a consumer sends a really emotional online message, it is better to leave these well alone. Whatever you try to do will be wrong. Companies which have a web-care team and already have considerable experience in Conversation Management almost always apply this golden rule. They see no point in reacting to vague, emotion-based insinuations from consumers.[178]

2 **Conversations between different consumers**
   If a number of consumers are discussing one of your products online, it is usually wiser as brand holder not to intervene.

This creates an unwelcome feeling amongst the consumers: rather like when you are talking to a group of friends and a stranger suddenly butts in.

3 Isolated negative experiences

Choose your battles carefully. Conversation Management is not the same as putting out fires. There are some discussions you can never win. Most web-care teams would agree with this strategy. Their experience shows that some people are so irredeemably negative that any reaction – no matter how well-meaning – is simply adding fuel to the flames.[179] This is not the opinion of Jaap Favier of the Forrester market research bureau, who says that non-reaction to online complaints is a sign of weakness. In his article in the NRC *Handelsblad*[180] he argues that companies should always give their consumers an answer. It is certainly true that it is always possible to give an answer, but this might not be the best way to avoid further negative word-of-mouth. By reacting to a small and insignificant incident, there is always a chance that you might turn a molehill into a mountain. This can only lead to greater amounts of unfavourable WOM. If you feel 'obliged' to answer this sort of contact, it is best to do it with an open question.

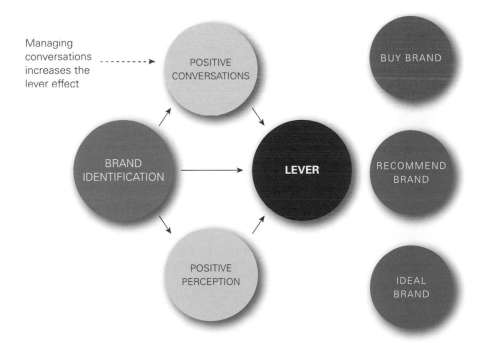

Bill Gates, Steve Jobs & Michael Dell

Bill Gates, the late Steve Jobs and Michael Dell have all been managers of high-technology companies, and are well-known as highly successful businessmen. But they have all taken a very different approach to Conversation Management.

Bill Gates does more or less nothing. Microsoft is – and will remain – a giant in the software industry. Until now, it has never seen its consumers as a partner, because it hasn't needed to. Even so, since the beginning of 2010 Bill Gates has been on *Twitter*. One day he had no fewer than 250,000 followers, which shows the enormous potential for Microsoft in Conversation Management.

Steve Jobs put the Apple brand on the map. This was a major achievement in its own right. Jobs was a typical conversation starter. He showed things and then put them into the hands of the Apple fans. They become responsible for the company's advertising through positive word-of-mouth.

Of the three, Michael Dell probably comes closest to being a true Conversation Manager. He switched his company onto this track during the Dell Hell crisis. Since then, he invites a hundred or so fans to visit his house each year, so that they can talk about the future of the brand.

Dell was one of the first companies in the world to manage conversations effectively. They began – as we all must do – by simply observing comments about their brand. The site *IdeaStorm* then smoothed the path for their conversations with Dell users. In no time at all, this site produced 10,000 new ideas, which were voted on by some 650,000 consumers.[181]

Since then, Michael Dell has built up a conversation partnership with some of his fans. These fans react to negative comments on the web. This makes the conversations more authentic than if Dell responds as a company.

As a result, negative word-of-mouth about Dell has fallen from an average of 60% to just 23%.[182] Convinced?

4 Conversations you don't feel comfortable with

If you are not certain how to react or whether to react, it is usually better to wait. As in conversation with friends and colleagues, you sometimes need a pause for thought, in order to find the best response. You have this same option in online Conversation Management: the right to remain silent. If you have this type of feeling with most of your online conversations, this probably means that you have not yet done enough observation. In this case, you must urgently invest more time in the monitoring of such conversations. This is the only way to gain the experience you need.

Not always necessary to answer

AS A MANAGER AS A BRAND AS YOURSELF

OBSERVE **FACILITATE** **PARTICIPATE**

Observation is a minimum requirement

A Conversation Manager participates

Once you are ready to participate in conversations with your consumers and know how to combine this with a new way of advertising, then you have become a Conversation Manager. Observing is without doubt the first important step. It is only when you feel able to participate in conversations with consumers in a fluent and effective manner that you are on your way to real Conversation Management.

A conversation can be started by the consumer or by you, as the representative of the brand: it makes little difference. If you regard every message that you send as the beginning of a potential conversation, then your activation will soon be transformed into a dialogue which will benefit both your brand and the consumer. In our marketing training, most of us were not taught how to conduct this kind of dialogue – yet it is essential, if we want to be successful in the modern market place.

The good news is that we already have a great deal of experience with conversations. We have them every day of our life: with family, with colleagues, with friends, with strangers. We have no 'problem' if we meet someone and just stop for a chat. It is the most natural thing in the world. Well, it is exactly the same with Conversation Management: you use the same skills and the same experience. Watch how you behave in your private conversations, and apply the same techniques in your conversations with consumers – and do it now! You will be amazed at the results.

THE KEY POINTS IN THIS CHAPTER

- The Conversation Manager has at his disposal *a methodology to manage his conversations with consumers*:

  1 *observing* conversations between consumers;

  2 *facilitating* conversations and;

  3 *participating* in conversations himself.

  There are many companies which see potential in step 3, but are not prepared to do much about steps 1 and 2. This is a mistake. You cannot converse with someone unless you have listened to them first and understand their language.

- *Observing conversations is in the* DNA *of a Conversation Manager.* Wherever he goes, he watches and listens to the different ways consumers talk. In addition, he regularly goes in search of interesting conversations on the internet. Last but not least, he sets up a structure which can regularly provide him with a detailed summary of the discussions being conducted by consumers with regard to his brand's sector.

- Facilitating conversations takes matters a step further. The Conversation Manager creates a platform on which consumers can offer their opinions and comments about the brand. *He encourages them to speak openly about his products.*

- Participation in conversations is the final step. For most managers, this is also the most difficult step, because it forces them to forget most of the things they have been taught about communicating as a company. *From now on, we need to communicate as people, not as companies – and this is can be very hard for a manager to do.*

- To summarize: the Conversation Manager manages conversations at three different levels: he observes like a manager, he facilitates through his brand and he participates as himself.

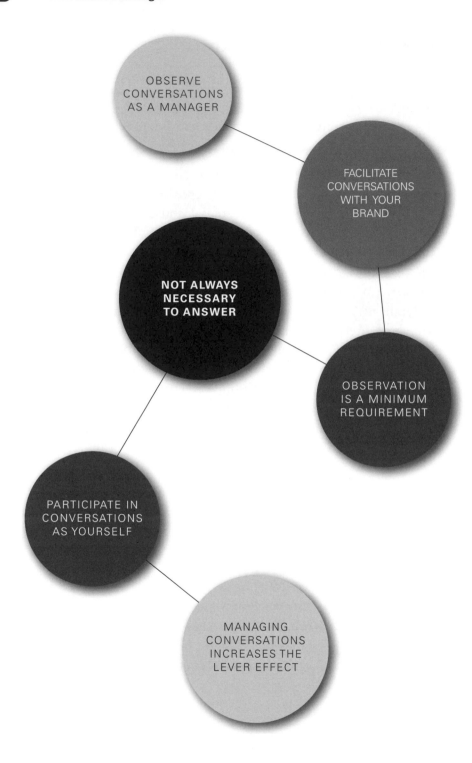

Part Three
I want to be
a Conversation
Manager!

PART THREE CONTENTS

Chapter Seven
The philosophy of the Conversation Manager

Don't do it for the wrong reasons

The first part of this book made clear that the philosophy of the modern consumer is no longer in keeping with the manner in which a traditional advertiser works. Sadly, however, many in the advertising business will try to cling to their old 'certainties' for many years to come.

In order to remain successful, brands will have to accept the need for radical change. Change is always difficult, but it is important to realize that this change should not be seen as threatening. On the contrary, it is the opportunity of a lifetime. Let us be clear on this: Conversation Managers are not only seeking to achieve short-term success. So make sure that you don't develop an interest in Conversation Management for the wrong reasons: for example, because it is 'cool' or because you 'don't want to miss the train'. Preparing a case for your brand as a one-off is obviously not a bad thing, but one swallow doesn't make a summer – and Conversation Management can offer you so much more.

In the previous Part I described the new frame of reference within which the Conversation Manager works: conversing with consumers on the basis of strong brand identification. These conversations can either be reactive (responding to the initiative of a consumer) or proactive (you initiate the conversation yourself). In this sense Conversation Management is a return to the age-old fundamentals of trade, but in a more volatile market than ever before.

This final part will be devoted to the practice of the theories contained in Part 1 and Part 2. We will be looking at how you need to adjust your company organization in order to make best use of Conversation Management; we will be suggesting how to freshen up your marketing policy; and we will provide you with a toolbox to help you reach both these goals. Finally, we will give you a simple 'to do' list which will allow you to take your first steps towards Conversation Management within 48 hours.

Strategy!

Conversation Management is more than just a clever tactic. It is a far-reaching change strategy. Conversation Management is a strategic domain within the field of marketing policy. To make this strategy easier to understand, this chapter will describe the five policy pillars on which your restructuring should be built:

1 Develop a structure to acquire continuous market insights.
2 Experience management is more important than product management.
3 Give something back to the consumers.
4 Position your consumers, not your brand.
5 The together-we-are-strong philosophy.

These five pillars will help the Conversation Manager to give shape to his frame of reference – his new way of thinking – within the company. All five policy pillars integrate ideas about brand identification, activation and the management of conversations. They transform the theoretical research contained in the previous chapters into hard commercial practice. You should regard these five strategies as the starting point of the change process for your marketing team.

Strategy 1. Develop a structure to acquire continuous market insights

The amount of available information over consumers has risen exponentially in recent years. The traditional market research methods of the previous decennia have certainly helped us to better understand

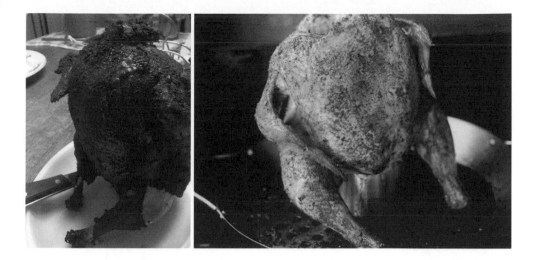

the consumer. These methods will continue to be important, but they are insufficient to offer the insights we need about the way the modern consumer thinks and feels.

The Conversation Manager builds a structure which allows him to collect insights about consumers on a continual basis. In addition to the information he receives from traditional research, he wants to know what is going on inside the consumer's head. What does he enjoy? What are his problems? What are his hopes? The Conversation Manager constantly monitors online and offline conversations, which provide him with input for his own thoughts, words and deed.

InSites Consulting once investigated the latest beer trends over a certain period of time for a brewing company. To do this, we monitored a considerable number of online conversations. Our customer was surprised – perhaps 'shocked' might be a better word – when we presented him with our final report. In the United States it was 'in' to cook 'beer-chicken' on the barbecue. *Flickr* was full of photographs of people who stuck a piece of chicken on top of a can of beer, and put them both on the griddle. In this manner, the chicken was steam cooked with a delicious beer taste! No one from the beer company had ever heard of 'beer chicken', whereas consumers in the US had been mad about it for ages.

This is a typical example. It is not instantly clear what a manager can do with a phenomenon as bizarre as 'beer chicken', but you at

---

Get to know Johnnie Walker and his friends

During the pre-Christmas period, the Johnnie Walker whisky brand organizes a major campaign to give its end-of-year figures a boost. These annual campaigns are based on the activation of the brand's 'ambassadors'. To make the plan work, it was necessary to have deeper insights into the target group. What are their interests, ambitions and opinions? To find the answers to these questions, a number of specimen consumers from the target group were followed online over a lengthy period. By looking at the sites they visited and analysing the information which they posted about themselves on the web, the company was able to build up a detailed and accurate picture about the 'friends of Johnnie Walker'. Watching people in this manner over a limited period can certainly be instructive for a specific purpose, but what a Conversation Manager really needs is a constant influx of observation results.

---

least ought to know that it exists. A few hours surfing the net would have been enough to gain this information, but in this case the trend only became known to the company because of an outside survey. Nothing further was done with this information, but one day an idea from one of your consumers may form the basis for a brand new production idea. To be sure that you don't miss this break-through idea when it comes along, you need to develop a new kind of structure. Finding an efficient way to check and monitor the lives of your consumers is a key challenge for the Conversation Manager. In Chapter 8 we will be examining a number of tools which can help you to meet this challenge.

In the future, our current market research instruments will no longer be sufficient to understand consumers fully.[183] There are, however, already a number of 'connection research' tools which can help. 'Connected research'[184] uses online platforms to map social inter-action between consumers. With this method, there is no real difference between the researcher and the consumer. Both have the same possibilities to contribute input. By making use of online com-munities, chat sessions and other interactive tools, this new type of research offers a series of deeper insights into consumers and their behaviour.

Strategy 2. Product management is dead. Long live experience management!

David Meerman Scott[185] describes it as follows: 'Nobody cares about your products (except you).' It is not satisfaction with your products which creates positive conversations, but rather the identification that people have with your brand.[186] Lifting the brand higher than the mere product level is therefore the Conversation Manager's challenge. The CEO of OgilvyOne, Brian Fetherstonhaugh, no longer believes in promotion campaigns in which the product is central. The P of 'product' is being replaced by the E of 'experience', according to this international bureau.

Energy giant Suez has understood what they mean. This is clear from a message which the company has been communicating to consumers since the middle of 2009. Suez wants to be the company that is concerned for our future. Their advertising makes no mention of their tariff systems, preferential or otherwise.[187] The only thing we are told is that we must opt for 'green' energy, if we want to make the future safe for our children. This storyline has given rise to much discussion amongst consumers, so that their brand does indeed rise beyond the product level.

Allowing consumers to feel or to take part in something that they can talk about is a further step in the creation of experiences.[188] Most people will be familiar with Coca-Cola's Christmas advertising. The same advert is broadcast each year and shows Coca-Cola lorries speeding through a wintery landscape. Not surprisingly, Father Christmas also makes an appearance. Of course, Coca-Cola lorries do ride through our land (through just about every land, in fact), and one Christmastide I came across a convoy of them: the sight instantly gave me a warm, seasonal feeling. I told this to my wife when I got home – and she was jealous that she had not been there!

The ultimate challenge is to create an experience which transcends the moment. The Redbull soapbox cart race, which is held each year throughout the world, is in keeping with this philosophy. Red Bull makes it possible for consumers to experience a fun-packed afternoon. Some teams prepare for months in advance, and the event leads to an active relationship with the brand over a longer period. This is exactly how you build brand identification.

Does this mean that products are no longer important? On the contrary, a high quality product continues to be an essential part of the consumer's positive experience. But it is no longer an end in itself. It has become a minimum condition of customer satisfaction. The objective of the Conversation Manager is not simply to have a good product, but also to develop a brand experience which will allow the consumer to talk about it in a positive manner to others. In this way, brand experiences become stories – stories embodying the six 'sticky' factors which strengthen activation.

InSites Consulting once organized a cooking workshop for a client, in which a number of leading chefs were persuaded to take part. Years later, I am still regularly asked about this workshop by other clients who have heard about it. We are a market research bureau: our products are statistics and insights. But in this instance we were able to create a brand experience which transcended the moment. And this results in positive word-of-mouth.

Learning from *The Fat Duck*

I am a gastronomy fan. Cooking at home, visiting restaurants, tasting fine wines: I love it all. Within the world of gastronomic restaurants, I am a big fan of *The Fat Duck*. This restaurant is located in the south of England, about an hour's drive from London, and has three Michelin stars – a very rare accolade. In fact, it is regarded as the second best restaurant in the world (although now that El Bulli has announced a fairly lengthy closure, perhaps *The Fat Duck* has become the best restaurant in the world).[189]

The food at *The Fat Duck* is a total experience. It is surprising, fresh, innovative, visually spectacular and a real treat for your taste buds. The menu guarantees you hours of pure delight. No fewer than 20 different delicacies appear on your table, and all of them are prepared to perfection.

Yet curiously enough, a week later you can hardly remember what you have eaten. The dishes are so numerous, the descriptions so complex: it is almost impossible to remember it all. What are the things that stick in your mind? Most of the women remember that they were given a special side table on which to place their handbags. Others remember the ice-cream with bacon and eggs. Everyone agrees that the ambiance is unsurpassed. These are the sorts of things which

people remember: not the product, but the story. The great food is just part of a great total experience.

The meals in the world's great gastronomic temples are invariably superb, but you can still leave disappointed if the quality of the food is not matched by the quality of the experience. Hence the trend in top restaurants to try and turn each dish into a 'moment to remember'. Surprises are built into the menus. Perhaps your salmon will be smoked at your table. Or aromatic oil will be rubbed onto your hand to improve the flavour of your meat. The number of possibilities is endless. But all these 'surprises' underline the equally surprising conclusion that even in the world's very best restaurants the food has become a minimum condition. The thing which really sets them apart as a brand is the quality of the experience they offer.

The Conversation Manager has the same challenge: to convince his team to create a good feeling, a good product and a total experience.

Strategy 3. Give something back

The modern consumer lives in an era when 'free' has become a part of our social context. Thirty years ago you almost needed to take out a loan to become the owner of an encyclopaedia. Today *Wikipedia* can be consulted for free by everyone. More and more services are being offered free of charge. This places an additional burden of expectation on companies. Consumers always want something 'a little extra' from their brands.[190]

There are many different ways to give something back to the consumer. Occasionally giving away a free gift is just one of the options. To celebrate Obama's election victory, Krispy Kreme UK[191] (a doughnut chain) offered a free cup of American coffee to every customer who came into the shop and shouted 'Yes, we can!'

Another possibility is working together with your consumers to support a good cause. Simply making a donation and announcing it in the press no longer has any real effect. People need to feel good, people need to experience. This means that it is better to work together to raise the money, preferably through a gimmick. Each year in April Ben & Jerry's organize their *Free Cone Day*. They give away a million free ice-creams to their customers. At the same time, they invite the organizations which support charitable works to collect in their shops. This means that these organizations get money directly from the people who enjoy the free ice-cream: a feel-good factor for all concerned!

Another example of this approach can be found with *Google*. In 2008 the search engine company launched the 10^100 project.[192] The project invited people to submit ideas which might help others. *Google* would then spend 10 million dollars on the best five projects. The *Google* users could choose these best projects by voting for their favourites from a list of 100 nominations. One of the ideas chosen was First Mile Solutions. The project installed wifi-apparatus on public buses.

This technology is capable of detecting and sending e-mails while the buses are driving through zones without an internet connection. This helps isolated communities in developing countries to keep in touch with each other through the net.

It may seem strange, but a third possibility to offer something back to your consumers is to recommend your competitors. Seth Godin[193]

Pepsi says goodbye to the Super Bowl and chooses to go online[194]

After 23 successive years of advertising at the Super Bowl, in 2010 Pepsi decided to spend its investment budget elsewhere: on the internet. TNS Media estimated that Pepsi spent an average of 33 million dollars each year on its adverts broadcast during this final game of the American football season (and one of the biggest sporting events in the world). 'In 2010 we have decided to change our marketing strategy. We want to focus less on a single event and more on a story and a continuous dialogue with our consumers,' said Nicole Bradley of Pepsi. As part of its alternative plan, Pepsi has allocated a budget of 20 million dollars to projects which can contribute to a better world. These projects will be chosen by the Pepsi public. At the beginning of January the company opened a website on which people could submit their project ideas. In February, people were allowed to vote for their favourite ideas.

Be careful if you want to give away a Hummer![195]

Giving things away to customers sounds like a very simple strategy, but it can sometimes go wrong. In 2006 McDonald's put a small toy – a Hummer – in each of its Happy Meals. General Motors wanted the parents of the Happy Meal children to have a more positive image about the Hummer car. But even before the action started, there was serious criticism. Environmental groups and parents were both unhappy about the Happy Meal plan. McDonald's reacted to the criticism with the following message on their blog: 'In the eyes of children these Hummers are just a toy. They do not see it as an attempt to get their parents to buy a Hummer or as a statement about the environment and the harmful emissions of vehicles.' When readers wanted to reply to this somewhat paternalistic message, McDonald's refused to post the negative comments. And so consumers expressed their dissatisfaction on a variety of other websites – loud and long.

described in his blog how he lost customers by failing to refer them through to his competitors. The through-referencing of customers in this manner is a unique way to strengthen your own brand. It gives you the status of being an expert in your field. You cannot help your customer in this instance, but you know the person who can. And so in his eyes you become the person who knows 'everything' about that particular sector. And who do you think he will come to when he next needs something from that sector? To 'his' expert, of course!

If a person steps into Burger King with a reduction voucher from McDonald's, the manager of the Burger King has a choice: he can accept the voucher, so that the customer stays and eats at Burger King, or he can show the customer the door (and the way to McDonald's). For a Conversation Manager this decision is quickly made: he has no problem accepting the voucher of his rivals. He knows that this will help to strengthen his own brand.

Zappos.com

Zappos.com is the largest online shoe store in the world. The company was set up in 1999. By 2008 it had realized a turnover of 1 billion dollars.[196] Zappos is built on the foundations of an iron-strong company culture. Each year they publish a cultural book in which the values of the company are reflected. Its strong and rapid growth is largely attributable to its customer-oriented approach in everything they do. On recruitment, every Zappos employee is given four weeks' training in customer service and friendliness. This training includes two weeks working in the company's call centre. Here they learn how to deal with real customers who call with real problems. At the end of the four weeks, the trainees have a choice: they can stay and work for the company, or they can leave immediately with a 2,000 dollar golden handshake: Zappos only wants staff who are motivated by the company ethos, not by money. Ninety-seven per cent of the trainees opt to stay. Impressive. Very impressive.[197]

The company's main driver is helping customers. This is evident throughout their activities, both great and small. Zappos never adds transport costs to its customers' orders. If they are not satisfied, customers can return shoes at the company's expense. If a particular style of shoe is not available, customers will be referred to a rival company which might have them in stock. The Zappos CEO encourages his staff to check at least five other websites during their calls with clients, to see if they can find the shoes they are looking for. Doing the right thing for the customer, giving them what they want, is the very clear philosophy on which the company's success is based. This has resulted in a Net Promoter Score of more than 75[198] and

phenomenal growth figures. In July 2009 *Amazon.com* bought the company for 800 million dollars. The guaranteed preservation of the company culture was made a condition of the sale.[199]

Strategy 4. Don't position brands, position people

We have already mentioned how modern consumers have become good marketeers in their own right. Using a variety of different channels, they have become experts at positioning themselves. The Conversation Manager searches for ways to allow his brand to play a role in the 'me'-marketing story of his consumers. A merchandizing strategy is one obvious option. Give the supporters of a football team a scarf and you assist in their personal positioning.

DangDang.com organizes 'lucky hour'[200]

During one hour each day, the online Chinese retailer DangDang.com gives away all purchases free of charge. If you press the 'buy' button during their 'lucky hour', you don't need to pay anything at all! Of course, they don't actually publicize the times of their lucky hours: this is something the customer has to guess! This may sound a very expensive way to give something back to consumers, but it is nothing in comparison with the number of new consumers which it helps to attract. Every consumer has to do the weekly shopping, so why not do it with the online store where you have a one in 24 chance of not having to pay?

Jaguar tried something similar a number of years ago, but soon found itself in the wrong lane. In 2001 this manufacturer of prestige cars decided to introduce a 'basic' model. The Jaguar X-type was intended as a rival for the BMW 3-series and the Audi A4. But who are Jaguar's traditional customers? That's right: older, well-off and well-established members of society. People who have positioned themselves very clearly. By launching this new 'downmarket' model, the company actually weakened the clarity of this positioning. Now there was a Jaguar available for 'just' 25,000 euros. This price did not match the image which 'true' Jaguar drivers like to have for themselves. By broadening the market, the company actually risked losing their core customers, who felt that their own image was being threatened. In the middle of 2009 Jaguar decided to stop production of the X-type.[201] It had learnt its lesson: position your customer, not your brand.

Strategy 5. Together we are strong

We know that consumers want to help us. They offer pro-active feedback to each other and to our brands. Allowing consumers to join in the design of advertisements or products help to increase their brand loyalty and commitment. In fact, according to Prahalad and Ramaswamy, co-creation with consumers is the way to the future for most companies.[202] Co-creation ensures that companies remain competitive, since their products are manufactured to reflect the needs of consumers in a way which they can understand and appreciate. In recent years, there have already been a number of instances of this co-creational process. For example, consumers have been asked to use their creativity to design adverts for their favourite brands. This is an interesting idea, but to date these efforts have been little more than one-off attempts to involve consumers in policy-making.

The objective of the Conversation Manager is to involve consumers in policy-making in a far more structured manner. Testing ideas on and accepting ideas from consumers is his natural reflex. This does not mean that the Conversation Manager no longer needs creative ideas of his own. However, these ideas should be focused on the activation process. Involving his brand's grassroots supporters is a key part of this process. If you involve them in the development of new products and advertisements, they will give their feedback with pleasure. Better still, bring them together in an online community. Regard these people as a kind of permanent sounding board, for the testing and receiving of new ideas (see the box on *myStarbucksidea.com*).

In this manner, Procter & Gamble created *Vocalpoint*, an online community for mothers where they could exchange ideas about the house, kitchen and garden. At the beginning of 2006, P&G decided to structurally involve this important target group of consumers in the development of its products. In the first instance, the company asked mothers for their opinion about the new Bounce dryer bar. In a relatively short period of time, 250,000 mothers logged on to the *Vocalpoint* site to give their feedback. The members of the community were given the opportunity to try out the new product before anyone else, providing that they were willing to share their feedback with the brand.[203]

The Conversation Manager dares to stick his neck out and go with the recommendations of his consumers. Asking their opinions and collecting their ideas brings with it a certain degree of obligation to do what they want. 'Involve your customers with your brand. If you do that correctly, it will result in increased loyalty and turn your customers into ambassadors for your brand. That is a powerful resource, but it also conceals a hidden danger – if you don't listen, things can soon go wrong,' says Johan Sanders of Sara Lee.[204]

If the consumer feels that something is being done with his ideas, he will become more committed than ever before.

MyStarbucks is open for new ideas

A successful example of the manner in which consumers can be structurally integrated into the development of policy is *MyStarbucksidea.com.* If you visit the website, you are greeted by the following invitation: '*You know better than anyone else what you want from Starbucks. So tell us. What's your Starbucks Idea? Revolutionary or simple, we want to hear it. Share your ideas, tell us what you think of other people's ideas and join the discussion. We're here and we're ready to make ideas happen. Let's get started.*'

The opinion of the consumer is central. Moreover, the invitation commits Starbucks to doing something about these opinions. This is the only way to convince the consumers that they are serious.

The site gives consumers the opportunity to put forward their own ideas and to vote on the ideas of others. Ideas which are voted as 'good' are then discussed in detail. This discussion often gives rise to even better ideas, which form the basis for change and innovation. The Starbucks web-care team takes active part in these discussions, to ensure that the ideas take sufficient account of the practical problems of implementation. The chances of a beneficial outcome are high, since the process reflects three crucial components for success: participation (open to everyone), recognition (voting on ideas) and collaboration (discussion of ideas).[205]

Next comes the implementation phase. Starbucks puts the ideas into immediate practical effect. Its innovation team communicates clearly on these matters via the site. The Starbucks VIP-card, free coffee for Gold-card members on their birthday and a free cup of coffee with the purchase of a bag of coffee beans are just some of the ideas which have been launched in this manner.[206]

During the first year of its existence, more than three million people visited this site. After six months, some 70,000 had already put forward ideas. Further proof that this type of initiative is much appreciated by modern consumers.[207]

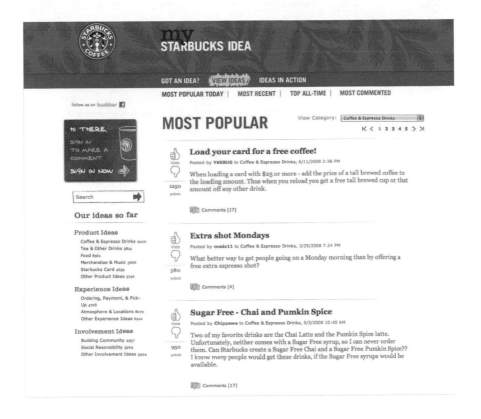

The Conversation Manager works together with the consumer

The strategies of the Conversation Manager make use of the fact that consumers have also become expert marketeers. By seeing the brand as a facilitator of positioning, he plays on – and to a degree exploits – the personal branding of his consumers. He also involves them in the development of new ideas (innovation, advertisements).

He helps his customers to experience something which gives them a story to tell. Stories create emotions and emotions bind the consumer ever tighter to the brand. In addition, the Conversation Manager also builds up a structure which allows him to catch the daily expression of consumer opinion in his knowledge net.

The Conversation Manager regards the consumers as being as important as himself. He understands these modern consumers and sees this as a great opportunity. As a result, the position of the consumer gains still further in importance. By learning how to take advantage of this development, he is investing in the future of his company. The four strategies outlined in this chapter will assist in the implementation of a new framework and a new way of thinking.

THE KEY POINTS IN THIS CHAPTER

- Conversation Management is not a tactical option, but a strategic choice for change in your marketing policy.

- Four strategies will make possible the implementation of a new framework and a new way of thinking in your marketing team. These strategies embody the philosophy of the Conversation Manager.

- There is so much information continually available in the modern world that it is essential to have a structure which can collect and process this information. It is a shame if new insights are lost because of a persistence in assessing information with outmoded techniques.

- Experience management is more important than product management. By providing the consumer with new experiences, you can increase brand identification and positive word-of-mouth.

- Give something back to the consumer. Consumers expect a lot from today's brands. Getting something for nothing is always popular. Working together for the benefit of a good cause is another option.

- Together we are strong. Involve the consumers in everything you do. Let them give feedback about advertising, new products and the general vision of your brand.

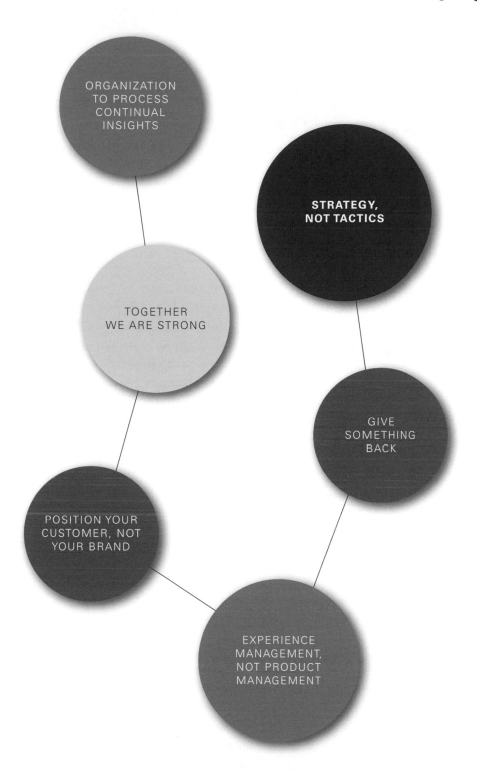

Chapter Eight
The Conversation
Manager in practice

The practice

The main objective of the Conversation Manager is to involve people in his policy by managing conversations with and between consumers. This results in a high level of brand identification, which in turn leads to good sales figures. The previous chapter discussed the strategic consequences for a company of following this change pathway. This should have made it clear that Conversation Management is a strategic story. It necessitates a number of structural investments and changes. This chapter will describe the nuts-and-bolts of the Conversation Manager's job. We will look in detail at the changes which need to be made to your marketing plan. Lastly, we will equip you with a practical toolbox which will make it easier for you to observe your consumers.

Changing the marketing plan

The daily activities of a marketing team should reflect the contents of a strategic marketing plan. The drawing up of a marketing plan is an annual task which causes a great deal of stress and strain. In reality, however, very little is done with these plans in concrete terms. In many organizations, 'marketing plan' is simply another term for 'marketing budget'. However, a plan is – or at least should be – so much more than just a financial instrument. A marketing plan should be an implementation pathway for the realization of your strategic objectives.

The Conversation Manager takes his marketing plans seriously. A plan offers certain concrete guideline for the development of the brand identitiy.

When drawing up a marketing plan, the Conversation Manager takes account of three key criteria:

- **Choice of media**
  The Conversation Manager has an open mind and is prepared to use all the different forms of media. He knows how and why to apply each particular form.

- **Budget flexibility**
  In order to take advantages of opportunities when they arise, the Conversation Manager manages his budget flexibly.

- **Added value**
  His plan contains practical measures which will give added value to the consumers through his brand.

These three aspects are merged to create his annual marketing plan. This allows him to integrate Conversation Management into daily policy.

Choice of media: every medium has its value

In general, expenditure on traditional media is declining. Posters and cinema advertising have been finding it hard to compete in recent years.[208] Internet advertising is the only real growth area in the advertising sector. Even so, the 30-second advert is not dead, neither on the radio nor on TV. Newspaper advertisements still appear, and will continue to do so. These traditional media will survive and will be used, also by the Conversation Manager.

The classic media have the advantage of reach, spreading the brand message to a large public. However, the Conversation Manager is also open to new media, and understands the benefits they can bring. He makes his choices wisely. And the main criterion for his choice is that the medium must spread his message in a manner which accords with his basic philosophy: every message is the start of a potential conversation.

Can you launch a product without using the classic media? If your product is unique enough, this is certainly an option (remember the case of Kai Mook). But it will not work for every new innovation. For this reason, it is important to discuss the media choices for all your products. Looking critically at the strengths and weaknesses of the different channels of communication in each phase of the product cycle is a core task for the Conversation Manager.

Hundred to One:
a multi-media success story

Hundred to One (or *1 Against 100*, as it is known in some countries) is a worldwide television hit. In this programme, a candidate has to compete against one hundred other people. In order to win, he has to answer a series of questions correctly, which allows him to gradually eliminate the others (if they get the same question wrong, they automatically drop out). If the candidate can knock out all his opponents before he answers a question wrong himself, he wins – usually a pleasingly large amount of money. The candidate always has the choice per category of answering an easy or a difficult question. He also has a number of 'aids', which he can use to help him, if he doesn't know the right answer. Millions of people around the world love this game and play it enthusiastically from the comfort of their sitting room armchair.

At the start of 2009 Xbox decided to launch an internet version of the game. Participants take part in a real *Hundred to One* challenge online. This digital version has already been downloaded 2,500,000 times.[209] At peak moments as many as 100,000 people were playing the game simultaneously – a world record.

It costs you nothing to take part and the winner receives 125 dollars. Microsoft has completely underwritten the business model of the game through the negotiation of a substantial sponsoring deal. Sprint and Honda were the main sponsors, each paying a million dollars for the right to advertise on the site and to have regular in-game flash-ups of their brand names.[210]

How a vaccine can conquer a market
in just a year's time[211]

Another good example of Conversation Management is the launch of the Gardasil vaccine onto the Belgian market. This vaccine offers women protection against the human papilloma virus (HPV), the main cause of cervical cancer.

This new medication first became available in Belgium at the end of 2007. The target group was young girls between the ages of 12 and 18 years. Within two years the majority of girls within this age group had been effectively vaccinated. In short, the product was a bit hit. Its success was attributable to several factors. The willingness of the Belgian government to pay for the vaccinations certainly speeded up market penetration, but several different media also made valuable contributions.

The launch of the vaccine was widely reported on both radio and television, and in the newspapers. This created a good level of consumer conversation. Wherever you went, people – and women in particular – were talking about Gardasil. These discussions were dominated by one question: 'Is it right for me?' Radio, television and the newspapers all took up this question and each carried advertisements which clarified the situation. Thanks largely to this media support, product familiarity was soon running at over 80 per cent in the target group, a figure achieved in just a few weeks' time. The creation of conversations through the original pr-releases, combined with advertisements which kept the cycle of conversations turning, helped to achieve the desired result: both for Gardasil and for the young female population of Belgium.

Buy flexibility: the 20 per cent rule

A traditional marketeer writes his marketing plan in a rigid manner. At the end of the year, he makes an analysis of what has been achieved against his preset objectives, and at what cost. On this basis, he makes a new set of plans for the following 12 months. This plan is then presented to the company management, with a request to find the necessary budget. To make sure that this budget is sufficient, most marketing managers add on an extra 10 to 20 per cent. Once the plan is approved, the entire budget – with its extra 20 per cent – is then allocated to specific projects.

The Conversation Manager looks at his budget differently. He knows that the behaviour of modern consumers can often lead to unexpected surprises and opportunities in the course of a year. For example, consumers might come up with a brilliant new idea which needs to be exploited immediately. However, this costs money. If you need to go back to the management to ask for the extra cash, this costs time. And while that time is passing, the opportunity may be slipping away. To prevent this from happening, the Conversation Manager builds a degree of flexibility into his planning. This is particularly true in respect of his approach to his marketing budget. Instead of allocating every last cent to a specific project, he leaves 20 per cent of the budget unallocated. This 20 per cent can then be used flexibly, as and when the need arises. This goes against the principles currently operating in most companies, and so the Conversation Manager must have good reasons to justify his actions. Responding quickly to the needs of consumers must always form the core of these arguments. The 20 per cent rule buys flexibility – and flexibility, like time, is a precious commodity.

Leverage: with an outlay of just 28,000 dollars, Mentos created a value of a cool 10 million

In 2006 there was a major internet-hype relating to Mentos and Coca-Cola Light. A variety of films on the net showed how you could create a huge fountain, simply by dropping a Mentos mint into a bottle of Cola Light. The first of these films was launched by Fritz Grobe and Stephen Voltz, to the accompaniment of fun music and under the title: *The Extreme Diet Coke & Mentos Experiment.* Within two weeks it had been viewed by some 450,000 people.[212] By the middle of 2009 more than 10 million people had seen it. All around the world, people were trying the experiment for themselves. *YouTube* was flooded by a tidal wave of similar films.

Coca-Cola's reaction to the hype was negative. Coke's spokesperson, Susan McDermott, said: 'We understand that this experiment is entertaining, but we hope that people will drink more Coca-Cola Light, instead of playing with it like a toy. This messing about with Mentos is not really in keeping with the brand personality of Coca-Cola.'[213]

In contrast, Mentos welcomed the hype with open arms. They even encouraged consumers to make more films. Their sales figures rose significantly during the hype period, without their needing to do very much at all. Mentos has an annual marketing budget of 20 million dollars. They estimated the value of the hype at 10 million dollars. And their investment? Just a paltry 28,000 dollars, most of it spent on whipping up the internet frenzy to new heights.[214]

In this case two companies were faced with an identical situation. One company saw it as a threat, the other company saw it as an opportunity. The more talented Coca-Cola marketeers probably wanted to jump on this train as well. But they didn't do it. Too scared of management reaction? Or perhaps there was just too little flexibility in their budget? Mentos, a much smaller brand, did have the necessary flexibility – both in terms of thinking and of budget. They seized the opportunity with both hands. Buying flexibility is the perfect way to take advantage of unforeseen circumstances.

There was an amusing footnote to this story. A few months later Fritz Grobe and Stephen Voltz were recruited by Coca-Cola to develop creative ideas. They now travel around the world encouraging people to try and break the Diet Coke–Mentos world record... on behalf of the soft drinks giant!

Branded utility: added value through the brand

The Conversation Manager offers an added value to his consumers through his brand. This is known as branded utility. This involves the creation of a commitment through the use of the brand in a manner which strengthens the bond with the consumer. Actions can be

InSites Consulting thinks of your back

InSites Consulting is a market research bureau which seeks to excel through its customer-oriented approach. To demonstrate this in a concrete manner to our marketing colleagues, InSites Consulting offered a 'goodie bag' to participants at the Marketing Foundation Congress in 2007.
At the end of the congress each visitor was given a bag with products and gadgets to a value of 200 euro. The bags were quite heavy, and so we laid a bicycle relay system to carry the gifts to the delegates' waiting cars. Most marketeers were instantly able to appreciate the added value of this brand service! It is also a good example of how branded utility really works.

launched which create an immediate and obvious added value for the consumer. This encourages the consumer to put his faith in the brand. This in turn enhances brand identification.[215] Our *Future Talking* research study[216] revealed that branded utility is one of the things which consumers expect companies to provide. Using your brand to help or benefit your consumers should therefore be one of your key marketing objectives as a Conversation Manager.

The Lipton Ice Tea brand gave branded utility to its customers during the heatwave in Romania in 2008. It imported hundreds of spray installations to keep consumers cool whilst sipping their soft drink, proving that the company could provide refreshment in more ways than one! In a similar vein, some mobile phone operators install soundproof telephone cabins at festival locations, so that young people can phone home without actually letting their parents know where they are... These are two very different examples, but they both have an obvious added value for the consumers concerned.

Nike and iPod: a perfect marriage

In 2006 Nike and Apple launched a combined product. The combination consisted of an iPod Nano and a specially-designed Nike running shoe which offered joggers almost limitless possibilities. Once you begin to run, the iPod memorizes your route and works out how far and how fast you have run. These details can then be uploaded onto a website specifically designed for this purpose. In this way, the iPod becomes a kind of personal trainer, constantly monitoring your improvements and making adjustments to your schedule. If you want, you can even compare your stats with those of others who use the same tool, so that it works as a performance benchmark. It also means, for example, that if a sports club organizes a race, the runners no longer have to run together at the same time. They can each run when it is most convenient for them, and the iPod system notes and collates all the individual times.

This is a product which opens up a whole new world to the consumers who are able to afford it. It is a unique example of branded utility. Together, the iPod and the Nike shoes offer more than they were ever able to offer before as individual products. The real added value of this concept resides in the combination of automatic monitoring and social usefulness.

Your practical toolbox

Your marketing plan is not the only thing that you will need to change. The Conversation Manager must also learn how to use a new range of online tools, if he wants to observe his consumers properly. The following are all tools which you should consider integrating into your daily activities.

- **Blogpulse (www.blogpulse.com)**
  This site will tell you what percentage of blog posts have been devoted to a particular subject. For most brands this is expressed in thousandths. It is not so much the volume that is important, but rather the evolution over a period of time. If you see that the buzz about your brand is increasing, it is important to find out why.

- **Wikipedia (www.wikipedia.org)**
  Useful for keeping you up to date about what is being written and said about your own brand or competing brands.

- **Technorati (www.technorati.com)**
  This is *Google* for blogs. The system works in exactly the same way as *Google*, but it only searches for blogs. The site allows you to identify and follow interesting blogs in your sector.

- **Google Blog Search (blogsearch.google.com)**
  Exactly the same as *Technorati*, but made by *Google*. Sometimes the results of *Technorati* and *Google Blog Search* can differ. For this reason, alternating use is recommended.

- **Google Trends (www.google.com/trends)**
  This tool offers the possibility to follow trends in search terms. Search terms are the words typed in by *Google* users when they are trying to track down a particular subject. *Google* records the frequency of search, as well as the most recent upcoming items during the same period. It will also suggest possible explanations, if the search behaviour of consumers changes dramatically or unexpectedly.

- **Google Alert (www.google.com/alert)**
  You commission *Google* to send you a pro-active mail whenever anything new about a particular topic appears on the internet. This topic might be your own brand or a rival brand. You can set the frequency with which you wish to receive these mails (daily, weekly, etc).

- **YouTube (www.youtube.com)**
  Everyone knows *YouTube*, but from now on you should regard it as a vital tool in your job as a Conversation Manager. Just take a look and see what (and how much) is being said about your sector. You will be amazed.

- Facebook (www.Facebook.com)
  You can search for groups or fan clubs of your brand on *Facebook*. Are people talking about your brand? What are they saying?

- Flickr (www.flickr.com)
  This is the *YouTube* for photos. Typing in a brand name on *Flickr* is like setting off on an ethnic safari. Once again, you will be amazed to see what photographs people have linked to your brand. This will help you to better understand how and when your products are used, and what emotions they arouse.

- Twitter Tweetscan (www.tweetscan.com) *and* *Summize* (search.twitter.com)
  These sites allow you to search *Twitter* posts in real time. This is useful, for example, on the day of a product launch to see what people are saying.

- Getsatisfaction (getsatisfaction.com)
  This is the online location to discover everything that consumers are saying about companies and products. It is a summary of the feedback that has appeared on various social network sites.

- Alexa (www.alexa.com)
  This tool lists the most visited sites within specific categories, sectors or countries.

- Brandtags (www.brandtags.net)
  This site records consumer perception with regard to more than one thousand different brands. Everyone who visits the site is asked to give their opinion about one or more of the brands listed. This allows you to check how your products – or rival products – are really seen by the buying public.

The Conversation Manager is a busy person. This means that he needs to make his search for consumer insights as efficient as possible. As mentioned in the previous chapter, he needs to organize himself in a manner which allows him to receive and process a constant stream of information. In this respect, *Daily 2.0* is a possibility. This tool is almost made-to-measure for Conversation Managers. It provides a summary of all the relevant insights which you have already acquired through the other, above-mentioned tools. A quick glance at this site will tell you more and more about your consumers and their profile. It is a significant one-time investment (thereafter it is automatically updated) – but well worth considering.

The Conversation Manager...

The Conversation Manager has all kinds of practical tools stored on the desktop of his computer. This allows him to immerse himself one or two hours each day in the fascinating world of consumers. In addition, he builds sufficient flexibility into his planning, which enables him to react quickly whenever an opportunity arises. He will also ensure a good mix of media. His brand should not only assist consumers in their own positioning, but if possible should also offer them an immediate added value. The challenge is to creatively influence the lives of your consumers through your brand.

THE KEY POINTS IN THIS CHAPTER

- To implement the philosophy of the Conversation Manager in practice, you will need to *make a number of changes to your marketing plan*. Your choice of media will change and there will be a need for greater flexibility. Your plan must also find ways to give added value to your consumers.

- All the different types of media will continue to be important. *Mass media are still a part of the Conversation Manager's toolbox*. Other channels of communication can also be used.

- In order to react quickly to opportunities, you need sufficient flexibility. The Conversation Manager *blocks 20% of his marketing budget to take advantage of these opportunities when they arise*. In this manner, he 'buys' flexibility.

- A brand should offer added value to its consumers. The Conversation Manager sees *his brand as a way to help consumers improve their lives*.

- The internet offers a number of free tools which can help the Conversation Manager with his job. Use these daily – and get to know your consumers better.

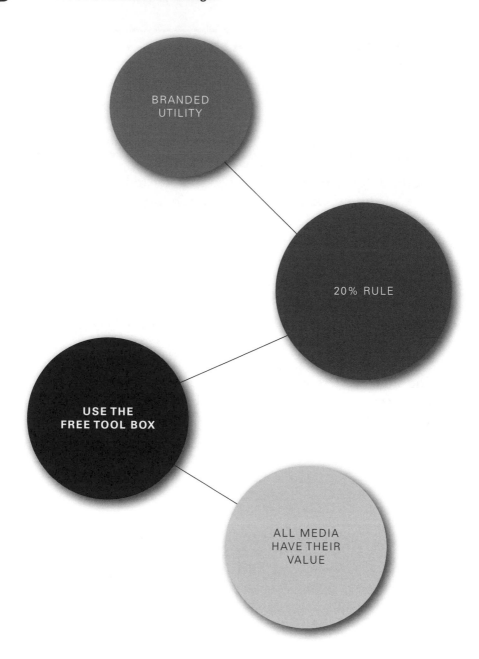

Chapter Nine
You have just 48 hours!

The spectre of ROI looms just around the corner

Don't kid yourself. If you want to apply the philosophy of Conversation Management in your company, you are going to meet a lot of opposition. Conversation Management means change, and people don't like change. So there will be plenty of your colleagues waiting to shoot you down. One of the most frequent criticisms will be that old favourite: *Return On Investment* (ROI). 'How will your philosophy help us? What does it mean in terms of the bottom line?' Of course, this is not an unreasonable question. At the end of the day, the changes you are proposing have to be to the financial benefit of your company. But this is precisely the object of the Conversation Management exercise – to bring stable, long-term growth. So try and persuade your senior management colleagues to look at ROI over a longer period, rather than focusing on short-term returns. There is no harm in short-term returns, but they are not necessarily a good basis for a sustainable future.

If you need to give your sales figures a quick boost, carry on applying the traditional methods of the past. If you organize a good sales promotion with the right advertising, then you will probably be able to make a quick profit. This is an excellent strategy, providing that you are prepared to change jobs every year. Good sales figures are always important for people who see 'job-hopping' as a career.

However, these old techniques will be of little use to you if you are more interested in building up a brand that actually means something, a brand that can survive and prosper without the need for a regular quick fix of one-off sales promotions. Only truly strong brands are in a position to do this: it is no coincidence, for example, that Apple is able to sell its expensive iPhones without promotional offers.

Don't try and look for an ROI in three months' time. The chance that Conversation Management will produce such short-term benefits is relatively small. It is the change process over a much longer period of time that will finally bear fruit – and yield profit. It is a bit like a snowball effect: it takes a while to get going, but once the momentum has gathered, it becomes almost unstoppable.

Your current position in the market will determine the speed with which results become tangible. If you already have high levels of brand identification, then it should not be long before you begin to see a positive return. If your brand identification is still limited, the results may take longer to appear. But appear they will: all it takes is a little time and patience.

Change begins with yourself

The philosophy of the Conversation Manager necessitates a new kind of relationship between your company and its consumers. This kind of change needs courage and persistence. Rome wasn't built in a day! It costs blood, sweat and tears – and this is what it will cost you, as well! So don't set the bar too high, at least not at the beginning.

Will you become a perfect advertiser if you train yourself to become a Conversation Manager? No! Advertisers have 50 to 60 years of experience of advertising on TV. Years of additional research have been carried out. Even so, from time to time they still manage to send out ridiculous – and commercially disastrous – spots. It is difficult to believe that after all these years there is still no watertight formula for the creation of a successful TV advert. But that is the reality of the situation – and everyone seems to accept it.

Conversation Management is a brand-new way of approaching your consumers, of talking to them. So far, little research into this new philosophy has been carried out. The group of Conversation Managers is still in the minority. This means that mistakes will inevitably be made. Companies will experiment with things that simply do not work. This is unfortunate, but not necessarily bad. Every investment which assists a learning process is a good investment.

Don't set the bar too high, we said – but don't set it too low either! You will not transform yourself into a Conversation Manager if you only apply 50 per cent of the philosophy. The different facets of Conversation Management all influence each other. Take one cog out of the machine, and the whole engine ceases to function. The bar must be set high for the implementation of the basic principles of the philosophy. Only set it lower when fixing the success criteria for individual actions within your broader framework.

Remember that change does not begin with the restructuring of your company or with a fine speech by your CEO. The truth of the matter was perfectly described more than 150 years ago by the great Russian writer, Leo Tolstoi: 'Everyone thinks of changing the world, but no one thinks of changing himself.' Believe in the story of the Conversation Manager and apply it wholeheartedly. Change begins with yourself.

48 hours to go

Do you recognize the following situation? You attend a conference and you are inspired by one of the speakers. On your way home in the car, you make your plans for the following day. You have heard a few ideas which may be useful for your company. The next morning you arrive at the office full of good intentions. But there are a hundred e-mails waiting to be answered and a dozen problems to solve. Before you know it, lunchtime has come and gone. In the afternoon, you get bogged down in a series of endless meetings. And it is the same story the next day, and the day after that. By the end of the week you hardly remember any of your good intentions from the conference. And so you carry on exactly as before... Is any of this sounding familiar?

My appeal is this: if you really believe in the story of the Conversation Manager and if you really want to apply the Conversation Management philosophy in practice, you must start within the next 48 hours! There is no room for delay. If you don't do it within the next 48 hours, you will never do it! Mark my words!

Most people postpone this change because it seems like a lot of work. But it isn't. Not really. By training yourself to become a Conversation Manager you will not need to work more. You will only need to work *differently*. Most of your tasks will remain the same.

But the way you organize and approach them will be different. It is not your hours of work that will increase, but rather the satisfaction and sense of achievement that you obtain from that work.

Your first 48 hours

Your transformation begins with a summary of all the things you want to change. The more concrete you are able to make this summary, the better it will be. To help you map out your change pathway, there now follows a specimen 10-point programme which can serve as your example. The programme contains three things that you need to do within the next 48 hours, and seven more that you can deal with in the days and weeks ahead.

1 **Understand your brand's current market identity**
   Conversation Management begins with the creation of good
   market identification. Having a correct insight into the current
   level of this market identification is therefore crucial for
   a Conversation Manager. This will allow him to assess whether
   his brand is built on solid foundations, or if he needs to rebuild
   these foundations from scratch.

2 **Observe**
   Surprisingly few advertisers follow conversations about
   their brand in a structural way. This can be a 'quick win' for
   a budding Conversation Manager. Use the tools described in
   Chapter 8 and set off on your own safari in the consumer
   jungle. Include some of these tools in your list of favourite
   internet sites. Find out all you can about your own brand and
   the brands of your competitors. Make it a habit to look at
   these sites regularly.

3 **Add flexibility to your marketing planning**
   Re-evaluate your marketing plan. How much room is there for
   flexibility? Do you have budget available to take advantage of
   unforeseen opportunities? If so, how large is this budget? What
   procedures or restrictions exist for its use? The likelihood that
   you will develop new ideas which need quick follow-up will
   grow as you increase your number of conversations. These
   ideas will cost money, so make space in your budget now!
   Implement the 20 per cent rule as soon as possible.

And afterwards? What else will change?

A number of other structural matters will also need to be changed. As soon as you have successfully completed the three tasks for the first 48 hours, move on to the following seven aspects of Conversation Management, which you can implement over a longer period of time (but not too long!).

4 **Cultivate fanship**
   The philosophy of the Conversation Manager is based on conversations between people about brands. A fan-base is of incalculable value for a company. Fans are your ambassadors. The Conversation Manager systematically builds a platform which allows him to communicate directly with his fans. Constructing this platform and maintaining the fan community are core tasks of the Conversation Manager.

5 **Use new performance indicators**
   The Conversation Manager is not only interested in knowing the reach of his campaigns. He also wants to know the level of activation (dissemination, creation) amongst his consumers. The Net Promoter Score must therefore be added to his list of indicators. Evolutions in the number and subjects of consumer conversations should be recorded in a conversation monitor.

6 **Facilitate and participate**
   Conversation Managers interact with their target group. In the first instance, they look to see how the brand can be used to encourage conversations. Next, there is the question of how they actually converse with their consumers. The general rule is: 'start slow, finish strong'.

7 **Let the consumer stand in your shoes**
   Invite consumers to send you new marketing ideas. Ask them what they would do if they were in your position. It is a simple matter to add this question to all your market research questionnaires. The Conversation Manager pro-actively searches for innovative ideas from his consumers. The web is a useful platform in this respect.

8 **Re-examine your relationship with your partners**
   Does your advertising agency fully support your new Conversation Management approach? If not, change them.

Look for a new agency which believes wholeheartedly in the modern consumer and the power of conversations. Make clear to the new bureau that you are not interested in building a new short-term market identity on the basis of viral campaigns. The three pillars of the relationship with your advertiser must be: long-term thinking, consistent implementation and consumer collaboration to promote the brand. Also make sure that your PR-bureau, your market research partners and any company which provides your market services all share this same philosophy.

9   Life is a safari
You need to recognize that you are now living in a safari park. Wherever you go, you will hear conversations. Observing consumers in their natural habitat is the Conversation Manager's favourite hobby. Climb down from your ivory advertiser's tower and immerse yourself in the consumer jungle. Make asking questions your second nature.

10 Missionary work
Finally, you must realize that you are a pioneer – and all pioneers are missionaries. Convincing others of the need for change is your task. You believe in the new consumer and the new approach, but you must make your colleagues and friends believe it too.

Once you have initiated these 10 steps you will be well on the way to becoming a Conversation Manager. But your fascinating journey is only just beginning. You have laid the foundations for a new way of advertising through conversations. You have applied the Conversation Manager's new way of thinking to all your marketing actions. It will still be some time before you have mastered the new philosophy completely, but after a while it will seem the most natural thing in the world. This is the moment when you can proudly say: 'I am a Conversation Manager!'

But even then, you have still not reached your final destination. You may have become a Conversation Manager, but there will still be some areas of your company where Conversation Management is not applied in full. For this reason our epilogue will describe the last stage in your journey: how to transform your company into a Conversation Company.

To round of our story, and also as a source of inspiration, I would like to end with two examples of the world's very finest Conversation Managers: Barack Obama (President of the United States of America) and Frank Eliason (Director of Digital Care at Comcast).

Obama: the turning point

The victory of Barack Obama in the presidential election of November 2008 was a historic moment in many respects. Perhaps most obviously, he was the first ever black president, a milestone event in the long history of his nation. But his election was also historic from a marketing perspective – because Barack Obama was the first politician of world stature to run his campaign like a Conversation Manager.

His basic philosophy was to involve people in his campaign, and thereby secure their commitment – and their vote. Instead of just having a few hundred campaign workers (the traditional approach), Obama wanted millions of campaign workers. Social networks were utilized to bring people closer to the president-elect. By becoming a 'friend' on *LinkedIn* or *Facebook* it was even possible to send a personal message to the Democratic candidate. This led to a positive spiral on the internet, and the figures were impressive.[217] Between the start of the campaign and his election as president, 13 million people had voluntarily registered on the e-mail list of his website. Obama had more than 3 million friends on *Facebook* and 5 million more on other social network sites. He uploaded some 2,000 films on *YouTube*, good for a total of over 80 million viewers.

The commitment which this created amongst these people was soon transferred into positive word-of-mouth. But the activation went still further. Three million of his biggest supporters donated money to his campaign fund.[218]

How is it possible to inspire such loyalty and commitment? During the campaign Obama was simply himself (or so it appeared). He was authentic. By communicating through social networks he extended his reach. As a result, his brand identification grew, so that his consumers were prepared to make ever greater efforts on his behalf. And to help this process along, he facilitated conversations. His site contained tools which could help site visitors to make their own blogs or videos. These visitors then used these tools to spread the Obama message. His own messages on social network sites were also the starting point for further discussions. Via *LinkedIn* he asked a series of questions about aspects of his policy. A politician who asked questions of the public? It had never been seen before.

Obama began on a small scale. He started his own website and observed conversations between the voters. In the second phase he made his own significant contributions to the content of these online discussions. This input was designed to stimulate yet more conversations. It was only during the third and final phase that he started to ask the public direct questions. If he had tried to do this straight away, the results would have been disastrous. Conversation Management is a process where it is crucial to follow all the steps in the right order. If you try to miss out a step, you will fail to reach your objective. Obama stuck to the classic Conversation Management trajectory: first he observed conversations, then he facilitated conversations and only then did he participate in conversations.

His authenticity received a further boost when he continued to pursue his Conversation Management strategy after his election. Via the site *organizingforamerica.org* the president invited the citizens of the nation to offer him advice on policy matters.[219] Via *Twitter* he encouraged the public to send messages to their senators if they were in support of a particular piece of legislation. This, he claimed, would allow the senators to know what the people were thinking, but indirectly it was proof that millions of ordinary citizens were still working for Obama. This is a very powerful activation tool.

Comcast must die: the story of Conversation Manager Frank Eliason

Comcast is one of the largest telecommunications companies in the United States. Amongst its many services, it offers cable television and internet solutions to its customers. Unfortunately, during 2007 44 per cent of these customers were unhappy with these services.[220] In particular, customer relations scored very poorly. The internet was awash with film clips which showed drunken Comcast staff visiting clients of the company, often falling asleep in the process.

In response to this sorry state of affairs Bob Garfield set up the website *comcastmustdie.com*. The mission of this site was to bring together dissatisfied Comcast customers, so that they could exert greater pressure on the company. Garfield's aim was not so much to bankrupt Comcast, but rather to bring about a change in its arrogant and overbearing attitude towards its consumers.[221] Within a matter of days, more than a thousand complaints against Comcast were posted on the site.

Comcast soon got wind of what was going on and decided to participate in the conversations. Frank Eliason was appointed as Director of Digital Care (although we prefer to call him a Conversation Manager). Frank went through the three classic stages of Conversation Management. First he observed and analysed the kinds of complaints which were being made online.[222] He also opened a forum on Comcast's own website, where customers could air their grievances directly with him. Finally, he began to reply to some of the complaints, effectively taking part in the conversations which he had helped to facilitate. He made use of all the available social media (*Twitter* in particular). Initially, he communicated under the ComcastCares-logo, but many consumers were soon asking who he was and why there was no photograph of him online. Frank adjusted to the new situation and did what the consumers expected of him. Each year he sent more than 100,000 personal messages to individual customers.[223] The fact that these people were now getting an answer was already a major step in the right direction – for both sides. One of the complaints he saw on *Twitter* said: 'Just telephoned Comcast customer-relations service. Not a pleasant experience.' His reaction was short and to the point: 'Can I help?'[224] In this simple manner he was able to participate meaningfully in the conversations of his consumers. It was nothing complex: he just tried to respond to their frustrations and help them where he could.

Two years later Bob Garfield wrote that the battle was not yet won, but that he felt things were changing at Comcast. 'They are more open to their customers and are trying to better organize their conversations with consumers.' Comcast, and most other major companies with it, is like a super-tanker: it takes a while before you notice that it has altered course. This gradually became apparent to the Comcast community, and as a result the relations between the company and its consumers were slowly rebuilt.

The wise Conversation Manager surrounds himself with staff who share his brand philosophy. It is this team which communicates directly with the consumers. The match between the members of the team and brand is the oil which lubricates the Conversation Manager's machine, and keeps it turning. Conversing with the public in this manner eventually becomes second nature. Together, the Conversation Manager, his team and the consumers are capable of building a powerful brand. Frank Eliason is leading just such a team, which monitors and implements the company's dialogue with its customers. And together they are indeed helping to recreate a strong Comcast brand. It is a perfect example of the Conversation Manager at work.

THE KEY POINTS IN THIS CHAPTER

- *Convince the senior management of your company* to invest in Conversation Management. Emphasize ROI potential in the long term.

- Change is necessary now, in order to remain successful. *Do not wait until the company changes, but start the process yourself.*

- Draw up a 10-point programme which maps out your change pathway in concrete terms.

- Within *48 hours* of reading this book you must implement the first three points of your programme. If you fail to do this, you have just been wasting your time.

- Complete your Conversation Management programme by implementing the seven remaining points in the days and weeks ahead.

- *Make Conversation Management your second nature.* Apply its principles consistently and you will experience more pleasure from your job. Once the results begin to come, there will be no stopping you!

47:59:59

IT BEGINS
WITH YOURSELF

Epilogue
The Conversation Company

This is just the beginning

Congratulations! You have taken an important step in your career.

The first step was the reading of this book.

The second step is your transformation into a Conversation Manager. By starting today with your change process, you can protect yourself against the threat posed by the new generation of advertisers (born after 1987).

But it doesn't stop there. The third step is to convince your team of the need for change.

And the final step is to persuade your company to embrace the new philosophy.

The conversation revolution is not just confined to the field of marketing. Almost every branch of the business world is in need of change. Your company must learn to evolve, if it wants to remain successful. But as we have already mentioned: change begins with yourself. And by reading this book, you now have a responsibility to change.

HRM is being influenced by our philosophy

After marketing, personnel policy is probably the area most affected by the implications of growing consumer influence. HR and marketing share many similarities. Internal communication relating to policy decisions is just as important as external communication with customers. The company's brand is also a powerful pole for the attraction of new staff talent.

HR managers are facing problems not unlike those of the traditional advertiser. Job candidates are overwhelmed with job ads which are based on the traditional advertising model. Fortunately, the Conversation Manager's way of thinking can also be translated into HR practice. A new-style recruitment campaign must give the potential candidates something to talk about. This will create interest in your company. By participating in the resulting conversations, your employer brand will increase in value.

Teenage genius teaches Morgan Stanley about social media[225]

In 2009 Matthew Robson was just 15 years old. He is living proof of the amazing insights which many young people of his generation possess. During his summer holidays, he did a work-experience vacation job at the Morgan Stanley Bank in London. At the end of his stay he wrote a report over the use of social media: *How teenagers consume social media*. This report has since become world-famous. CEO's in Tokyo, Wall Street and Europe are all talking about Matthew's conclusions. These include the assertion that young people use *Facebook*, whereas *Twitter* is for old people. Reading newspapers is a waste of time, since the news is bundled more efficiently and can therefore be read more quickly on the internet. Money can be a problem for young people and so they go in search of free entertainment. This results in the illegal downloading of video games, music and films. Radio is losing its popularity, since the youth of today prefers to choose its own music, which it listens to online or on the iPod. Out of the mouths of babes...

In addition, the arrival of the post-1987 generation on the work scene is also an opportunity for companies. Select new people who have the competencies necessary to implement your new change policy. Recruit this young talent into your company: it can only help speed up the necessary transformation process. You will be surprised by what they have to offer. Develop new training and education programmes which reflect their way of life.

The new generation needs a different type of guidance and mentorship. They grew up in a world where the giving of instant feedback was the norm rather than the exception. This is what they expect from their managers once they start work: instant feedback. Supplement traditional coaching methods with the new possibilities offered by modern communications. For example, a company in the marketing sector recently launched a 'happiness-index' for its office. When turning off their computer, every member of staff has the opportunity to register a score on a five-point scale to indicate how happy they felt that day. By collating all the scores, the HR department can gain an idea about the working atmosphere in the company. This type of instant assessment mechanism is popular with the new generation. Remember to praise their creativity, their flexibility, their multi-tasking and their communication skills during your job evaluation discussions with them – and hold these discussions regularly.

Give these young people the freedom they are looking for. Offer them a flexible remunerations package. Ask what type of rewards interest them the most. They are all different and want to be treated differently.

Finally, an appeal to HR managers: do not get all agitated about the use of social networks at work. They are not the source of mischief and laziness which most of you seem to think. If you discover misuse, you should search for the problem in the person concerned or in your own recruitment and training procedures. *Facebook* and *Twitter* are not to blame.

R&D gets an experience focus

The Conversation Manager wants to create experiences for his consumers. Consumers enjoy these pleasing experiences, which give them something to talk about with their friends. This book has described in detail how traditional marketeers are much too focused on products. But this problem actually starts with the research and development process. The R&D departments work hard to devise new technological developments, and these developments are inevitably expressed in terms of new product concepts.

In view of the importance of experience marketing for the modern consumer, the R&D departments will have to learn to devote more of their resources to this new trend. This means spending more time and more money on the creation of valuable experiences. As always, the right balance needs to be struck. New top-products remain an important pre-condition for the continued long-term success of the company, but the development of such products must now take account of the need to have an experience-based component which can satisfy the emotional requirements of consumers – and therefore help to cement brand identification. This is the real future of R&D.

Market research needs reinventing

The market research department is also starting to feel the impact of the new consumer. It is the task of this department to 'understand' these consumers, to acquire new insights into the way they think and feel, so that the rest of the company knows how to approach them.

A market researcher faces exactly the same problem as the advertiser. The level of participation in market research is falling. In this respect, the techniques used to collect data bear a strong similarity to the traditional advertising model. They just send out a 'message' – in their case, a questionnaire – to the consumers and hope that the consumers can be bothered to answer.

The future of market research will be very different. Research information will be gathered by analysing existing data (ie observing conversations), so that traditional field work will no longer be necessary. This new technique will provide 'answers to the questions we do not yet have'. Of course, companies will also require an answer to the questions they *do* already have, but this will rely increasingly on the goodwill of the respondent. This goodwill can be created by using the philosophy of the Conversation Manager. A good method is to give something back to the consumer (eg feedback from the company about decisions taken on the basis of the research). If you can find a way to enhance their experience and increase their brand commitment, they will provide the necessary information with pleasure.

CRM is dead

During the last Womma conference in November 2008, everyone was in agreement that relationships with customers are central to the generation of word-of-mouth. This same message was proclaimed 10 years ago, when Customer Relationship Management (CRM) was introduced. But it is now clear that word-of-mouth is a much improved version of CRM.

Why is it an improved version? Because with WOM the focus really is on the customer, and not on a sophisticated software package.

- CRM is often equivalent to little more than the sending of personalized messages to customers.
- CRM is about databases, WOM is about talking to people.
- CRM is a separate department within a company, whereas WOM is everybody's responsibility.
- CRM has call centres which reel off pre-formatted questionnaires to customers, whereas WOM is about real conversations between real people.
- CRM sends messages to customers, WOM listens to what they have to say.
- CRM speaks about A-customers, WOM speaks of customer advocates.

It is true that there are many similarities between the two systems, but WOM is more authentic and more personal than CRM ever was.

A good example of this new form of CRM is the site *KraftFirstTaste.com*. This is an initiative which allows selected customers the first opportunity to try new Kraft products. These products are delivered to their homes, where they can test them on themselves and on their families, long before they are available in the shops. Afterwards, they can tell Kraft about their opinions and experiences. This is the right way to create brand advocates. In similar fashion, Michael Dell invites a large number of his company's brand advocates to his home each year, where they can brainstorm about the future of their brand: word-of-mouth marketing in its purest form!

Join in the conversation...

If you would like to convince others of the need for change in today's company structures, why not surf to **www.theconversationmanager.com**. Here you can find an up-to-date selection of new case studies which show where Conversation Management has succeeded (or failed). There is also the chance to post your own examples: perhaps your story is the inspiration that someone has been waiting for.

Join in the conversation and convince your colleagues and friends to become Conversation Managers. It is our only way forward. Good luck!

References

1 Lazarsfeld, Berelson, Gaudet, *The People's Choice*, 1944.

2 *Internet World Stats*, data from March 2009.

3 Goldsmith & Horowitz, 'Measuring motivations for online opinion seeking', *Journal of Interactive Advertising*, 2006.

4 InSites Consulting, *Word-of-mouth research*, 2008, confirmed by Edelmann's trust barometer.

5 Semantic Wave 2008, report: *Industry roadmap to web 3.0 & multibillion dollar market opportunities*, Mills Davis, Project 10X's.

6 Tim Berners-Lee, *Weaving the web*, 1999.

7 Semantic Wave 2008, report: *Industry roadmap to web 3.0 & multibillion dollar market opportunities*, Mills Davis, Project 10X's.

8 Jop Esmeijer, 'Web, Webbier, Webest: from 1.0 to 3.0 and beyond', *Frankwatching*, January 2009.

9 InSites Consulting, *Patient Health Study*, 2009.

10 InSites Consulting, *Patient Health Study*, 2009.

11 Paul Dunay, 'Social Search: could it be a Google Killer', *Social Media Today*, June 2009.

12 Eric Schonfeld, 'The future of social search (or why Google should buy Facebook)', December 2008.

13 Womma, definition Word-of-Mouth, 2005.

14 InSites Consulting; KellerFay; Weber, *Boomers big on word-of-mouth*, 2007; 'What's all the buzz about? Everyday communication and the relational basis of word-of-mouth and buzz marketing practices', *Management Communication Quarterly*, 2006; 'Information search in virtual communities: is it replacing use of offline communication?' *Journal of Marketing Communications*, 2006.

15 Salzman, Matathia & O'Reilly, *Buzz. Harness the power of influence and create demand*, 2003.

16 InSites Consulting, MC DC *research*, September 2009.

17 InSites Consulting, MC DC *research*, September 2009.

18 With thanks to Tom De Ruyck and Dado Van Peteghem for the inspiration.

19 Adam Singer, *Thefuturebuzz.com*.

20 InSites Consulting, MC DC *research*, September 2009.

21 Seth Godin, *Purple Cow*, 2002.

22 Union of Concerned Scientists website.

23 Joseph Jaffe, *Life after the 30-second spot*, 2005.

24 InSites Consulting, MC DC *research*, September 2009.

25 'Stampede on the internet', *De Standaard*, 27 June 2009.

26 *blogpulse.com*

27 'Internet gradually becoming the only new source', *De Standaard*, 23 June 2009.

28 'Rats take over Kentucky Fried Chicken', *De Standaard*, 24 February 2007.

29 'Taco Bell and KFC: not so YUM-my?', MSN *Money Central*, February 2007.

30 *Wikipedia* articles over *Wikipedia* and *Encyclopaedia Britannica*.

31 Dave Evans, *Social Media Marketing*, 2008.

32 Surowiecki, *The Wisdom of Crowds*, 2004.

33 Dan Hill, *Emotionomics*, 2002.

34 Martin Lindstrom, *Buy-ology*, 2008.

35 InSites Consulting, MC DC *research*, September 2009.

36 *Wired*, 2009.

37 'Kodak's social media success', Altitudebranding.com, September 2008, Ambur Naslund.

38 Robert Scoble and Shel Israel, *Naked Conversations*, 2006.

39 InSites Consulting, MC DC *research*, September 2009.

40 Fons Van Dyck, *Het merk mens*, 2007.

41 InSites Consulting, MC DC *research*, September 2009.

42 Levine e.a., *The Cluetrain Manifesto*, 2000; Orr, 'Parsing the meaning of web 2.0', ABA *Banking Journal*, 2007.

43 Etcoff, Orbach, Scott & D'Agostino, *Beyond Stereotypes: Rebuilding the Foundation of Beauty Beliefs*, 2004.

44 *Contexts.org*, Dove versus Axe.

45 *Wikipedia*, The Million Dollar Homepage.

46 Forrester Research, *Media trends, time spent on the internet continues to grow*.

47 'eBay buys Marktplaats for 225 million', *webwereld.nl*, November 2004; 'Has eBay paid too much for Marktplaats', *marketingfacts.nl*, November 2004.

48 InSites Consulting & Vlerick Leuven Gent Management School, *Mixed mode buying research*.

49 *Bring back the love, the break up, YouTube*. Search: bring back the love Microsoft.

50 'Rounding up the buzz... Will one Chicago Woman's Tweet cost her $50.000?', *Chicagonow*, July 2009.

51 Joseph Jaffe, *Join the conversation*, 2007.

52 Boris Nihom, 'Listen to this', SWOCC, 2009.

53 'How two Coke fans brought the brand to Facebook fame', *AdAge*, 16 March 2009.

54 Joachimsthaler & Aaker, 'Building brands without mass media', *Harvard Business Review*, 1997.

55 Gross Rating Point (GRP) is a figure which combines reach and selectivity. It is a term used by the media to express advertising impact.

56 Himpe, *Advertising is dead, long live advertising*, 2006.

57 InSites Consulting, *Digital Media Mapping*, 2007.

58 *Americana persona, The history of advertising*, Wordpress.com.
59 Conversation with Peter Quaghebeur, director-general, Vmma.
60 InSites Consulting, MC DC *research*, September 2009.
61 T-Mobile 'Dance', integrated campaign, Case Study, www.utalkmarketing.com.
62 KellerFay Group.
63 IAB *advertising revenue report*, PWC, 2009.
64 IAB *social advertising, best practices*, May 2009.
65 Levine, Locke, Searls & Weinberger, *The Cluetrain Manifesto*, 2000.
66 InSites Consulting, MC DC *research*, September 2009.
67 Co-creation with Lego, www.brickmeetsbite.com.
68 *Daily Mail*, August 2009.
69 Dunkin Donuts' *Facebook* campaign turns your profile pic into prizes, mashable.com, June 2009.
70 InSites Consulting, *Branding & Advertising study*, 2008.
71 Carol Nader, 'Generation Y: complex, discerning and suspicious', *The Age*, 9 October 2003.
72 InSites Consulting, *Youth Online study*, 2007.
73 InSites Consulting, *On Screens study*, 2009.
74 InSites Consulting; KellerFay; Weber, *Boomers big on word-of-mouth*, 2007; 'What's all the buzz about, everyday communication and the relational basis of word-of-mouth and buzz marketing practices', *Management Communication Quarterly*, 2006; 'Information search in virtual communities: is it replacing use of offline communication?', *Journal of Marketing Communications*, 2006.
75 Steve Jobs vs Obama, mashable.com, Ben Parr, January 2010.
76 InSites Consulting, *ConAir, WOM research*, 2008.
77 Keller, 'A turning point for word-of-mouth marketing', opening speech at the Womma Summit in Las Vegas, 2007.
78 InSites Consulting, *ConAir, WOM research*, 2008.
79 Rosen, *The anatomy of buzz*, 2000.
80 InSites Consulting, *Carlson relationship monitor*, 2008.
81 InSites Consulting, *A new approach for measuring 'buzz'*, Esomar paper, 2007.
82 Fishet, *Brand logo recognition by children*, 1991.
83 McNeil, *Kids as customers*, 1992.
84 InSites Consulting, *Branding & Communication research*, 2008.
85 David Meerman Scott, *World Wide Rave*, 2009.
86 InSites Consulting, *Digital Media Mapping*, 2008.
87 'Baby Kai: an elephant worth its weight in gold?', *Het Laatste Nieuws*, 19 May 2009.
88 *rainforest-alliance.org*.
89 InSites Consulting & Boondoggle, *Conversations mapping research*, 2008.
90 Wavemetrix, *Online buzz report Apple iPhone*, January 2007.
91 Reichheld, *The ultimate question: driving good profits and true growth*, Harvard Business Press, 2006.

92 Kumar, Petersen & Leone, 'How valuable is word of mouth', *Harvard Business Review*, 2007.

93 Marsden, Samson & Upton, *Advocacy drives growth*, London School of Economics, 2005.

94 Keiningham, Cooil, Andreassen & Aksoy, 'A longitudinal examination of Net Promoter and Firm Revenue Growth', *Journal of Marketing*, 2007.

95 BMC, *Churn index survey*, 2007.

96 Ledbury research, 2006.

97 'People lie about holidays', *Spitsnieuws*, July 2009.

98 Al Ries & Jack Trout, *The 22 immutable laws of marketing*, 1994.

99 Susan Fournier, 'Consumers and their brands: developing relationship theory in consumer research', *Journal of Consumer Research*, 1998.

100 Martin Lindstrom, *Brand Sense*, 2005.

101 Choice, *Airline satisfaction survey*, 2007.

102 'Donaldson shows Mickey the door', *Het Nieuwsblad*, 19 December 2007.

103 'Donaldson goes bust', *Trends*, 22 October 2008.

104 Susan Fournier, 'Consumers and their brands: developing relationship theory in consumer research', *Journal of Consumer Research*, 1998.

105 Interbrand, *Best global brands*, 2008.

106 Martin Lindstrom, *Brand Sense*, 2005.

107 *allfacebook.com*.

108 Fitzsimons and Chartrand, 'Apple's logo makes you more creative than IBM's', *Journal of Consumer Research*, 2008.

109 Brand Asset Valuator.

110 Aaker, *Building strong brands*, 1995.

111 Keller, 'Brand synthesis: the multidimensionality of brand knowledge', *Journal of Consumer Research*, 2003.

112 Dye, 'The buzz on buzz', *Harvard Business Review*, 2000; Reichheld, 'The one number you need to grow', *Harvard Business Review*, 2003.

113 Friedman, Schillewaert, Ahearne & Lam, *Brand leverage study*, InSites Consulting & Houston University, 2009.

114 Rudy Moenaert, *Visionaire Marketing*, 2003.

115 Cutting Tiger Woods generates positive buzz for brands, *Adweek*, December 2009.

116 *clubbrugge.be*.

117 'Audi is the most popular brand with Belgians', *De Standaard*, 8 May 2009.

118 Harley Davidson, *Annual Report*.

119 KellerFay WOM research.

120 YouTube video: Domino's pizza turnaround.

121 Lodish & Mela, 'If brands are built over years, why are they managed over quarters?', *Harvard Business Review*, 2007.

122 Malcolm Gladwell, *The Tipping Point*, 2000.

123 InSites Consulting, *A new approach for measuring 'buzz'*, Esomar W3 Conference, 2007.

124 KellerFay Group & BzzAgent, *It's what they do, profiling word-of-mouth volunteers*, 2007.

125 Womma, *Measuring word-of-mouth: current thinking on research and measurement of word-of-mouth marketing*, vol. 1, 2005.

126 InSites Consulting, *A new approach for measuring 'buzz'*, Esomar W3 Conference, 2007.

127 InSites Consulting, *Word-of-mouth research*, 2008.

128 *ExpoTV survey*, 2009.

129 InSites Consulting, *A new approach in measuring 'buzz'*, Esomar WM3 conference, 2007.

130 Wikipedia Google web-quest Da Vinci Code.

131 About.com advertising cases.

132 'Naked truth about the brand king', *The Guardian*, 27 July 2002.

133 De Pelsmacker, Geuens & Van den Bergh, *Marketing Communications*, Prentice Hall, 2001.

134 Burger King under fire for Whopper Virgins taste test challenge, *Telegraph*, December 2008.

135 Engelland, Hopkins & Larson, 'Market mavenship as an influencer of service quality evaluation', *Journal of Marketing*, 2002. Lyons & Henderson, 'Opinion leadership in a computer-mediated environment', *Journal of Consumer Behaviour*, 2005. Boris Nihom, 'Listen to this!', SWOCC, 2009.

136 Boris Nihom, 'Listen to this!', SWOCC, 2009.

137 InSites Consulting, *A new way of measuring 'buzz'*, Esomar WM3 conference, 2007.

138 Seth Godin, *The Purple Cow*, 2002.

139 Rogers, *Diffusion of Innovations*, 2003.

140 Moore, *Crossing the Chasm*, 1992.

141 Franzen & Van den Berg, *Strategisch management van merken*, Kluwer.

142 Fournier, 'Consumers and their brands: developing relationship theory in consumer research', *Journal of Marketing*, 1998.

143 *Website analysis of car brands*, Belgian website, 2007.

144 Anderson, 'Customer satisfaction and word-of-mouth', *Journal of Services Research*, 1998.

145 KellerFay, 'Influencers are essential in driving WOM and affinity with the brand', *Admap*, April 2009.

146 Brown, Barry, Dacin & Gunst, 'Spreading the word: investigating antecedents of consumers' positive word-of-mouth intentions and behaviours in a retailing context', *Journal of the Academy of Marketing Science*, 2005.

147 Research by KellerFay & InSites Consulting.

148 KellerFay.

149 InSites Consulting, MacBase post testing TV campaigns, 2010.

150 Joseph Jaffe, *Join the Conversation*, 2007.

151 InSites Consulting & Goodyear, *Pre-test viral campaigns Goodyear*, 2007.

152 Molson photo contest brews up anger, *Globe & Mail*, November 2007.

153 Molson ends Facebook campaign after complaints, Bloombert.com, November 2008.

154 'Island caretaker job offer: get paid 150K to swim and snorkel', *Mex Cooper*, January 2009. 'Best job ever', eleftheria parpis, May 2009.

155 'Heineken breaks digital responsible drinking campaign', *Marketing Magazine*, November 2008.

156 *wikipedia.org*, search: coke zero (English).

157 InSites Consulting, *ConAir WOM tracker*, 2007.

158 'The Blair Witch Project, 10 years later', *Entertainment Weekly*, July 2009.

159 BoxOfficeMojo, 2006.

160 'When fans hissed, he listened', *Chicago Tribune*, 2006.

161 Heath & Heath, *Made to stick; why some ideas survive and others die*, 2007.

162 InSites Consulting, *Evolution of Beauty, Dove case study*, Esomar Berlin 2007.

163 Salzman, Matathia & O'Reilly, *Buzz, Harness the power of influence and create demand*, 2003.

164 InSites Consulting, *Future Talking*, 2008.

165 Wansink & Van Ittersum, 'The perils of plate size: waist, waste & wallet', *Journal of Marketing*, 2008.

166 'Goodies in small packages prove to be a big hit', *The New York Times*, 30 May 2005.

167 *InSites Consulting*, social media research 2010.

168 David Meerman Scott, *World Wide Rave*, 2009.

169 Wind, Mahajan & Gunther, *Convergence marketing; strategies for reaching the new hybrid consumer*, 2002.

170 Fournier & Lee, 'Getting brand communities right', *Harvard Business Review*, 2009.

171 Adformatie, June 2009.

172 Ford bets the Fiesta on social networking, Wired.com, April 2009; Ford Fiesta Movement: can social media sell cars, mashable, October 2009.

173 Levine, Locke, Searls & Weinberger, *The Cluetrain Manifesto*, 2000.

174 Patricia Swann, 'The Kryptonite lock-picking incident', *Cases in Public Relationship Management*.

175 Lydia Polgreen, 'The pen is mightier than the lock', *New York Times*, 17 September 2004.

176 Case study: Dell Hell, Kimberly Williams, 2010.

177 *www.gertje.info*.

178   Linda Volkers, *Reageren of niet? Afwegingen bij online reputatiemanagement*, Jungle Minds.

179   Floor Van Riet, 'Web-care: strengthening image and reacting effectively to complaints', *Frankwatching*, January 2009.

180   'First-aid for web discussions', NRC *Handelsblad*, January 2009.

181   Andy Sernovitz, *How Dell turned around negative word-of-mouth*, March 2009.

182   'What's the Dell position on social media?', *marketingfacts*, April 2009.

183   Forsyth, Galante & Guild, 'Capitalising on customer insights', *McKinsey Quarterly*, 2006.

184   Schillewaert, De Ruyck & Verhaeghe, 'Connected research', *International Journal of Market Research*, 2009.

185   David Meerman Scott, *Word Wide Rave*, 2009.

186   InSites Consulting, *Brand leverage research*, 2009.

187   OgilvyOne Worldwide CEO keynote speech at AdTech: 'Four Es, not four Ps'.

188   Transumers report, *Trendwatching.com*.

189   The S. Pellegrino world's 50 best restaurants list, 2009.

190   Free Love report, *Trendwatching.com*.

191   Generation G report, *Trendwatching.com*.

192   'Google project 10,100', *Dutchcowboys.nl*, 30 September 2008.

193   *Seth's blog, how to lose*, October 2008.

194   Pepsi turns ad focus online, espn.com, December 2009.

195   Recent advertising flops and why they failed, about.com, August 2006.

196   *About Zappos.com*

197   'Why Zappos offers new hires 2,000 dollars to quit', *Business Week*, September 2008. Bill Taylor, 'Why Zappos pays new employees to quit, and you should too', *Harvard Business Publishing blog*.

198   Speech Tony Hsiech at the Womma conference, November 2008, Las Vegas.

199   'Amazon steps into Zappos' shoes', *eMarketer*, 24 July 2009.

200   Trendwatching.com, Generation G, February 2009.

201   'Jaguar stops production of basic X-type model', *De Standaard*, July 2009.

202   Prahalad & Ramaswamy, *The future of competition*, Harvard Business School press, 2004.

203   Vocalpoint.com, 'P&G turns to its vocalpoint.com to learn what mom would say', business courier, July 2009; 'P&G and vocalpoint want your voice', crowdsourcinglinks.com, February 2009.

204   'Co-creation? The time is ripe, now for the mentality', *Frankwatching.com*, 26 June 2009.

205   Charles Leadbeater, *We-Think: mass innovation, not mass production*, 2008.

206 'MyStarbucksIdea – more than 70,000 ideas', *weexperience.nl*, July 2009; *blogs.starbucks.com*.

207 'Mystarbucksidea – is it working?', *Web Media Rite*, January 2009.

208 'Spending on advertising continues to fall', *De Standaard*, July 2009.

209 *1 Against 100* hits 2.5 million downloads, Shacknews, August 2009.

210 New technology enables thousands of people to play simultaneously using the Xbox Live online gaming network, Ben Fritz, June 2009.

211 Conversation with Sabien Deboodt, Sanofi Pasteur MSD.

212 Erwin Boogert, 'Explosive Mentos sweets are big internet hype', *Emerce*, 13 June 2006.

213 Suzanne Vranica, 'Mixing Diet Coke & Mentos makes a gusher of publicity', *Wall Street Journal*, 12 June 2006.

214 Suzanne Vranica, 'Mixing Diet Coke & Mentos makes a gusher of publicity', *Wall Street Journal*, 12 June 2006.

215 Brian Morresey, 'Digital design goes well beyond websites', *Adweek*, March 2008.

216 InSites Consulting, *Future Talking*, 2008.

217 Edelman, *The social pulpit: Barack Obama's social media toolkit*, 2009.

218 'Obama raised over $500 million during campaign', *Huffington Post*, November 2008.

219 'Obama announces "organising for America"', *Washington Post*, January 2009.

220 'PR nightmare: "Comcast must die" blog unifies angry customers', *livingstonbuzz.com*, 6 December 2007.

221 Bob Garfield, *The Social Customer Manifesto*, 2007.

222 'Comcast Cares: social media interview with Frank Eliason', *online marketing blog*, 15 December 2008.

223 Speech Frank Eliason to the Womma conference, Las Vegas, November 2008.

224 'Comcast's Twitter man', *Business Week*, 13 January 2009.

225 'Twitter is for old people, work experience whizz-kid tells bankers', *Financial Times*, July 2009; 'Fifteen-year-old analyst thinks Twitter is past it', *De Standaard*, July 2009.

About the author

Steven Van Belleghem is also the author of *The Conversation Company*. He is one of the Managing Partners at InSites Consulting and a part-time Marketing Professor at the Vlerick Business School. His passion is for helping clients with strategic and tactical issues around conversations, word-of-mouth and social media.

Together with the team at InSites Consulting, he helps companies to get a grip on current consumers through branding, advertising and integrating conversations in their entire company strategy. As an author and Marketing Professor, he also lectures and teaches throughout the world on conversations and social media.

About InSites Consulting

InSites Consulting was established in 1997, and although a marketing research company, the founders never really wanted to be market researchers. InSites Consulting really is a crazy blend of academic visionaries, passionate marketers and research innovators that are determined to challenge the status quo of marketing research.

Over the last 10 years the company has grown at an amazing rate of 35 per cent per year. Today there's more than 130 employees working in five offices (BE, NL, UK, RO, US) getting their energy from helping world-leading brands to improve their marketing efforts and to develop deeper connections with consumers on a global scale. InSites Consulting has been rewarded with no less than 15 international awards.

The recipe for success: a never-ceasing enthusiasm, a lot of hard work, a culture of sharing, and permanent innovation in research methods and marketing thought leadership. And last but not least: positively surprising clients every day.

More information on **www.insites-consulting.com**.

Index